ESSENCE: EXPLORING SPIRITUALITY

This course is not designed to tell the whole Christian story, or necessarily to lead people to a point of Christian commitment. Our hope is, however, that *Essence* will stimulate many who take part to begin to explore Christian spirituality. It should be seen as the first stage of a journey to a fulfilling and enriching way of life, not the final destination.

Statement of Responsibility

We wish to inform all leaders and participants undertaking this *Essence* series that Share Jesus International as the originator of *Essence* accepts no liability for any direct or indirect injuries caused, either physical or psychological, during any of the sessions.

Local leaders are responsible for the implementation, safety and welfare of their group sessions. We strongly urge local leaders to provide and use some form of eye protection when engaging in the tile exercise during Session 4.

essence

ROB FROST

KINGSWAY PUBLICATIONS
EASTBOURNE

First published 2002
Reprinted 2003

ISBN 1 84291 111 2

Published by
KINGSWAY COMMUNICATIONS LTD
Lottbridge Drove, Eastbourne BN23 6NT, England.
Email: books@kingsway.co.uk

Book design and production for the publishers by
Bookprint Creative Services, P.O. Box 827, BN21 3YJ, England.
Printed in Great Britain.

Contents

Acknowledgements

Sincere thanks goes to the following people who have been involved with the development of Essence over the past two years:

Mr Hugo Anson; Marian Arthur; Lou Ashford; Ms Liz Babbs; Revd David Banbury; Mr Jonny Baker; Jacky Barker; Guy Bridgewater; Roland Bryan; John Burns; Antony Chant; Revd David Currie; Louise Donkin; Professor John Drane; Revd Canon Robert Freeman; Andy Frost; Jacqui Frost; John Graystone; Revd Irene Greenman; Sue Griffiths; Tracy Harding; Doug Harris; Sheila Hendley; Richard Herkes; Marten Holmes; Revd Graham Horsley; Mr Daryl Jackson; Peter Jeffery; Jean Kerr; Jonathan Kitching; Angela Knowles; Paddy Lane; Revd Piers Lane; Revd Freddie Latham-Durrant; Steve Lindridge; Alex Lydall; Revd Canon Roger Matthews; Margaret McVeigh; Andrew Meredith; Lieut. Colonel Alex Morrice; Claire Newby; Alan Poole; David Pott; Mr Howard Ross; Revd Malcolm Rothwell; Roy Searles; Michael Shrubsole; Angela Smith; Revd Briant Smith; Mr Richard Smith; Jon Turner; Christopher Webb; Ms Sylvia Wooton.

Many others were also involved in the pilot sessions themselves and we are grateful for all their support.

A special thank you goes to Jacqui Frost and Angela Smith for piloting the final Essence series at the Lantern Arts Centre. To Claire Newby for editing the final draft of the manual and to Alex Lydall for editing the second draft.

Special thanks also goes to the following team of people for the production of the Essence CD: Paul Field (Producer); Liz Babbs;

Claire Newby; Rob Lacey and to Trevor at Premier Radio for help in research.

Thanks also to Eagle, ICC, Proost, Kingsway and Sparrow for granting us permission for the use of music on the CD.

We wish to acknowledge, with sincere gratitude, grants given towards the pilot phase of this course from the Board of Mission of the Anglican Church and the Baptist Union of Great Britain.

Introduction

Whether we like it or not, New Age thinking and spirituality is now very much part of mainstream Western culture. The Henley Centre Report called 'The Paradox of Prosperity' indicates that around a quarter of all UK adults are currently seeking to renew their spiritual life.

Every day thousands of people engage in activities that they see as 'spiritual'. Aromatherapy, personal development, green spirituality, astrology, tarot and alternative medicine are just a few of the activities that can become gateways into an exploration of spirituality. Sadly, this road that many are following may lead to an exploration of New Age spirituality, but doesn't give an opportunity to discover the riches of Christian spirituality.

The church seems to be largely disconnected from this massive hunger for spirituality. Many Christians are struggling to find ways of interfacing with this hunger.

It is even more worrying that some committed Christians are finding these new 'pick 'n' mix' forms of spirituality appealing. Many are finding that institutional Christianity seems spiritually dead. It does not feed their hunger for personal spiritual renewal.

Essence is a creative response to this rising hunger for spiritual renewal. It has been developed over a two-year period and has involved hundreds of participants. Its style is laid-back and non-threatening.

We started with a theological exploration involving Professor John Drane and around 20 Christian leaders actively engaged in mission in a New Age context. Next we consulted with a group of Christians who would consider themselves 'in touch' with New Age thinking and with the culture of spirituality we were trying to interface with. Many of the concepts featured in this book started here.

Later we called together about a dozen mission enablers from different Christian backgrounds who shared our concerns. We persuaded them to take the programme ideas already formed and to pilot them in towns throughout the UK in the autumn of 2001. Following detailed feedback, the *Essence* series was completely rewritten.

Finally, a team at the Lantern Arts Centre did a full pilot series in Wimbledon in the early weeks of 2002, and the material was reworked again.

At every phase of the development of *Essence* two things have amazed me. First, how hungry committed Christians are for something less cerebral and more experiential in their faith. Time and again, in developing these materials, Christian participants have been overwhelmed by the presence of God and moved to tears by the depth of sharing they experienced. Many have said that they have found *Essence* stimulating and refreshing.

Second, I have been fascinated to discover how open people are to what we have on offer in *Essence*. One lady in her sixties who attended our Wimbledon series said, 'I have been into Buddhism and Eastern religion for many years, but I have never encountered anything as rich as this. You've challenged all my preconceptions about Christianity. And the love here. I've never known anything like it.'

If, as a leader, you embark on this series, you're not taking an easy option! I'd certainly encourage you to join one of our training courses. My book *A Closer Look at New Age Spirituality* could be a helpful introduction to this whole area of interest.

Essence involves a great deal of preparation and careful organisation for each session. I do believe, however, that it could be one of the richest experiences of Christian fellowship and mission you've ever encountered.

Revd Dr Rob Frost
Director, Share Jesus International

Leaders' Guidelines: an Overview

The *Essence* spirituality series is a new tool for Christian mission. It is designed to introduce people who have an interest in spirituality or in New Age philosophy to the Christian faith. It is not exclusively for non-Christians, however. We have discovered that a wide range of existing Christian fellowship groups have benefited enormously from the *Essence* experience.

We recommend that there should be a minimum of three Christian leaders for every series, with at least one leader for every six participants present. As long as there is sufficient space, there can be as many as 40 participants, with about seven leaders.

The series runs over a six-week period and covers a wide range of topics. Alternatively, it could be used over a residential weekend from Friday to Sunday. *Essence* aims to give an experiential introduction to the Christian faith in a culturally relevant way. Each week the programme takes participants on a journey of self-discovery as they investigate Christian perspectives through different activities. The overall objective is to encourage all of the group members to make a personal journey towards God. This 'hands on' approach encourages individual participation. The series takes popular concepts from New Age spirituality and refocuses them from a Christian perspective.

The series should not really be held on church premises. The best setting might be a lounge area in a gym, library or pub. It should be made clear on advertising material that it is based on Christian spirituality. It should be advertised alongside the New Age series in coffee shops, New Age shops, health centres, libraries, etc. Leaders should aim to reach those who would never enter a church. The course should take place in an informal setting with comfortable seating and low lighting.

Participants are expected to pay for the sessions in the same way that they would pay to enrol on a secular course. The fee is used to cover the costs of the materials and room hire.

The series is very practical, so casual clothing is recommended. It might also be helpful if participants brought a large cushion or beanbag for use in relaxation and meditation.

The key feature of the series is the small group work, which is referred to in the manual as a 'set' (usually five or six participants and one leader). Participants should be encouraged to move around into different sets each week as this will help to broaden the range of shared experiences for the participants. One or more leaders could share the responsibility for leading the series.

Leaders' Guidelines: Participants

To ensure that your *Essence* series is successful it is important that some basic guidelines are set in place. These guidelines are designed to safeguard the leaders and the group members.

- The group must ensure that confidentiality is maintained at all times. Anything shared by anyone within the group should never be shared outside of the group. Make it clear that participants should feel free to share personally or equally to refrain from sharing, whichever they choose. There should be no pressure to share anything personal at any time. The group must accept the guidelines on confidentiality from the very start of the series.

- Respect for one another and for one another's views is essential. Listening to each other's options in a non-judgemental way is of paramount importance for the success of the programme.

- There should be an opportunity for people to stay behind after the sessions if they wish to chat further with the leaders about any issues raised.

- Don't put stringent time limits on people's creative responses, work or discussion in the sessions. Allow more time for this if needed. Participation is the key to a good *Essence* course.

Leaders' Guidelines: Sessions

- Each session should take approximately one and a half to two hours in total. People might like to spend time chatting and chilling out afterwards, so leaders should allow some extra time for this important aspect of the *Essence* experience.

- Leaders should spend time together ahead of the sessions in order to go over the material involved to ensure that they all understand the format of each session. The set leaders must understand their roles. In the manual we have included a shopping list at the end of each session. This should help leaders to prepare the required materials. It is important to bear in mind that planning and preparation takes time.

- *Essence* should be run as informally as possible. Leaders are advised to use the crib sheets that are located at the end of each session. These are a helpful way of quickly identifying the running order of the sessions rather than having to use the whole manual.

- It would be useful for the leaders to have read the book *A Closer Look at New Age Spirituality* by Rob Frost for background information. This is especially important if group members are coming to *Essence* with an interest in New Age spirituality.

- The setting for *Essence* should be as informal as possible. Each week the leaders should set out the room so that a relaxed atmosphere is created, for example by using comfortable chairs, large cushions, beanbags or mats, and creating plenty of space for people to be able to spread out. The use of low lighting can also help to create atmosphere. This should be done before the group arrives.

- Relaxing music should be playing in the background as people arrive. Group leaders should be present to welcome the participants to the session.

- The 'sets' referred to in the sessions are small groups consisting of no more than five or six members. Each set should have its own leader who has been briefed on the activities for that session. Each set activity is symbolised by ☺.

- When the session leader asks the sets to feed back to the larger group, the set leaders should ask different members of the group to report back each time so that everyone feels involved.

Notes on meditation (by Liz Babbs)

Christian meditation is a form of prayer that can lead to direct communion with God. It is not focused on experiences or requests, but on surrender. We are learning the simplicity of being with God and enjoying his presence. It is not an intellectual exercise.

To quote Dietrich Bonhoeffer:

> *Just as you do not analyse the words of someone you love, but accept them as they are said to you, so accept the Word of Scripture and ponder it in your heart, as Mary did. That is all. That is meditation.*

There are many references to meditation in the Bible, particularly in the Psalms.

> *Blessed is the man . . . [whose] delight is in the law of the Lord, and on his law he meditates day and night. He is like a tree planted by streams of water, which yields its fruit in season and whose leaf does not wither. Whatever he does prospers.*
>
> (Psalm 1:1–3)

In the book of Joshua, God commanded Joshua to meditate:

> *Do not let this Book of the Law depart from your mouth; meditate on it day and night, so that you may be careful to do everything written in it. Then you will be prosperous and successful.*
>
> (Joshua 1:8)

Christian meditation is not like other forms of meditation because it does not require us to empty our minds and hearts, nor does it encourage a preoccupation with self.

Notes on journalling (by Liz Babbs)

Keeping a journal is an important part of the spiritual journey. A diary can help us to organise our time, but a journal runs alongside time and reviews it. It helps us to get in touch with our inner and outer world. You write in a journal in the way you might talk to a close friend, recording thoughts, feelings, words, pictures and Scripture, etc. Writing things down is not only therapeutic, it helps to clarify issues. All you need to get started is a notebook and pen.

Keeping a journal is a contemplative way of asking key life questions:

- Where am I now?

- Where have I come from?

- Where am I going?

- Where would I like to be going?

A journal is a confidential record of our spiritual growth and an ongoing dialogue with God.

Participants of *Essence* are encouraged to write a journal during the six-session programme, but it is not compulsory!

Notes on the Ignatian form of reflection (by Malcolm Rothwell)

An 'Ignatian' contemplation is a form of prayer recommended by Ignatius of Loyola. It consists of taking in a scene from the life of Christ and reliving it. You imagine that you are actually in the scene as events are occurring and you are a participant. The process is best explained by way of an example.

Read a passage of Scripture such as the story of Martha and Mary in Luke 10:38–42. Then spend some time quietening yourself in preparation by doing an awareness exercise. For example, be aware of your breathing and know that God is closer to you than your breathing.

Next, imagine that you are in the home of Martha and Mary. Can you describe the home? What is it like? Is there a fire? Furniture? Are there any animals around? How big is it? Is it tidy? Clean? Are there any smells? How many rooms are there? Is there an upstairs? What is the weather like?

Now imagine Jesus coming into this house with some of his disciples. What is the atmosphere? Where have they come from? Are they tired? Hungry? Thirsty? Is there much conversation?

Try not to look at the scene as an observer, but imagine that you are actually present in the home of Martha and Mary. What are you doing there? What are your feelings? Are you in the same room as Jesus, or in the kitchen? Do you speak to anyone? If so, to whom? Do they reply? What are you feeling?

After spending some time in this scene spend a few more moments in the presence of Jesus in quiet prayer before slowly returning to the room in which you began the exercise. In your own time open your eyes. Be aware of the people around you and be aware of yourself, whispering your own name to yourself. In other words, spend some time coming back to your own situation.

Note that this kind of contemplation is not easy and is not for everybody. It may be a case of 'if at first you don't succeed then try again'. You will probably fare better at a second attempt.

Some people object to this form of contemplation, saying that it is not a theological or an historical way of approaching the gospel narratives. It is, however, a means of entering the text in a mystical way. It is one way of making the text come alive and, for many people, it works. By being present at the scene and by identifying with one of the characters (e.g. Martha, Mary, a disciple, a bystander), participants become aware of their own feelings and what it means to be present with Jesus.

Of course the meditation has to be entered into with an attitude of faith, in the belief that God only desires that which is good for us, and that God is ready to speak through our hearts. In this attitude of exploration you are in a position to attain the truth of mystery.

Key to Symbols

☺ Set sections

▷ Choose one of two options

📖 Things to do before the next session

♪ *Essence* CD can be used here

✾ Optional section

The Journey So Far

Key concepts: bonding, belonging, community, touch, spiritual highs and lows

The aim of this session is to encourage people to focus on their journey through life, and to consider the spiritual dimension of life. The Christian theology underpinning this session teaches that God knows us and loves us and is with us throughout all of our life experiences. He can help us in the difficult times and rejoices with us in the good times. We can hand our past hurts over to him.

Introduction to the journey

People arrive and are welcomed by the group leaders.

> See Leaders' Guidelines at the beginning of the manual.

1. *Food*

Different kinds of bread (e.g. naan, ciabatta, unleavened) and dips (e.g. guacamole, sour cream and chives) are laid out at the side of the room and people are invited to share the food together. Assorted drinks such as flavoured mineral water and fruit juices are also available. The group is encouraged to eat throughout the evening whenever they feel like it.

Leaders' Notes

Leaders may feel that they would like to provide a meal before the first session. If so, please remember to create something that is easily eaten, such as pizza. A vegetarian option should also be made available.

2. *Journey to the session*

Members of the group are asked to turn to the person next to them and to share about the journey they made getting to the session. They are asked to recall as much information as possible, including what they saw, what they felt, their emotions and how they felt on their arrival. From this starting point, the group is encouraged to share about how little we take notice of the details of life around us. We often walk around with our senses closed. During *Essence* we hope to open up our physical awareness, as well as our spiritual awareness.

3. *The cord of belonging*

Group members are each given a length of string, ribbon or cord approximately 50 cm long and invited to form sets of no more than five or six.

See guidelines on 'sets', p. 15.

Each set is seated in a circle, with people keeping hold of their piece of string. After everyone has shared their name, the set leader poses the following questions:

- What groups do you belong to?

- What does it feel like to 'belong'?

- Do you enjoy belonging?

This section is aimed at helping the group to get to know each other and to bond as a community. They are encouraged to recognise that they are a part of unseen groups, e.g. people they live next to or people they share an office with.

The session leader explains that this session is the foundation of a new group that hopefully will become close over the next few weeks and which may bond into a kind of community. To symbolise this link the group members are invited to tie the ends of their string with a reef knot (so that it can easily be undone) to their neighbour's string. They then lay the circle of string on the floor in front of them.

Leaders' Notes

During the introduction to Section 3 the leaders may hand out a variety of cord, ribbon or string. Having a variety means that the participants can choose their preferred colour or type.

4. *Guidelines*

The sets reconvene in the larger group and the leader sets out some guidelines for the *Essence* series.

> See Leaders' Guidelines: Participants for details.

5. *Massage/touch*

The leader who introduces this section should make everyone feel at ease and give permission for people to opt out of this activity at any point they might choose.

> ### Leaders' Notes
>
> Leaders should be aware that some people do not like to be touched. It should be made clear that the participants can opt out of this section at any point. As an alternative they might like to massage their own shoulders instead.

Each set forms a circle and participants are invited to take part in a simple massage activity. The massage we recommend is as follows:

Watching the seed as it grows

- Place an imaginary seed in the centre of your neighbour's back. (With the point of your finger place the seed in the centre of the back.)

- Cover it with soil. (Move your hands slowly inwards from the outside edges of the back.)

- Pat the soil down gently. (Gently pat the back.)

- Sprinkle it with the rain. (Move fingertips down the back.)

- Let sun shine upon it. (Use palms of the hands to make circle movements.)

- Watch it grow up really strong. (Move your palm up the spine slowly.)

- The flower has now grown up, and is ready to pick. (Pick the flower.)

- Turn around and give it to the person behind you to say thank you!

This activity is to help the group to bond together and to relax, and to give people an awareness of the importance of the sense of touch.

The journey to here

6. *Sharing*

The leaders could take this opportunity to introduce themselves and to share a bit about their lives and the meaning and importance of spirituality to them. They should also try to reiterate the importance of belonging as a personal experience for them.

7. *Individuality*

As a way of moving the group on, the leader can explain that they are made up of a collection of individuals who have travelled different journeys and that each has something unique to contribute. The leader then asks the group members to untie their piece of string/cord as a sign of their individuality within the group. This string/cord should be retained for a later exercise.

8. *'Stones' meditation*

See Leaders' Guidelines: Sessions, under 'Notes on meditation'

Everyone takes a pebble from a pile of pebbles in the centre of the room and the music starts. Each person finds a comfortable spot to sit or lie down while holding the pebble and exploring it visually and physically. This activity resonates with the 'touch' theme. The 'Stones' meditation,

track 1, should be played from the *Essence* CD. Alternatively, a leader could read the 'Stones' meditation over relaxing background music.

Stones

Think of your favourite beach and visualise yourself lying there. The pebbles are gently moving as the waves lap onto the shore. See the colours all around you – reflected in the sea . . . the shells . . . the sky . . . And now feel the warmth of the sun on your body as you relax into the warm sand beneath you. [Pause]

Now imagine that you have become one of the pebbles on the beach. How does it feel to be gently lifted up as the waves lap over you – refining . . . smoothing . . . redefining? [Pause]

Enjoy the rhythm of the sea washing over you as you breathe out anxiety . . . and breathe in peace. [Pause]

Now think of those times when the tide of your life's circumstances has smoothed away your own rough edges. [Pause]

Entrust yourself into the loving arms of the one who gives us the gift of his rest. [Let music play out]

© Liz Babbs 2001

9. *Getting lost and being found*

After the meditation it is important that people are not made to feel that they have to sit up. One of the leaders simply moves into a time of Christian testimony in which they share their own faith story. They talk about their highs and lows, the good and bad times and the dark and light experiences of their life. This links the 'Stones' meditation to a more personal reflection on how life shapes and changes us and how it can make us more rounded and whole as people.

Throughout the session the group will be focusing on the road they have travelled on their journey through life. The meditation passage used as a basis for this is Psalm 23.

The journey of life

10. *Psalm 23*

At this point Psalm 23 could be used. Play track 2 on the *Essence* CD: 'The Lord's my Shepherd', by Stuart Townend, with vocals by Joanna Hogg. The words of this song are as follows:

> *The Lord's my Shepherd, I'll not want.*
> *He makes me lie in pastures green.*
> *He leads me by the still, still waters,*
> *His goodness will lead me home.*

> Chorus:
> *And I will trust in you alone.*
> *And I will trust in you alone,*
> *For your endless mercy follows me,*
> *Your goodness will lead me home.*

> *He guides my ways in righteousness,*
> *And he anoints my head with oil,*
> *And my cup, it overflows with joy,*
> *I feast on his pure delights.*

> *And though I walk the darkest path,*
> *I will not fear the evil one,*

For you are with me, and your rod and staff
Are the comfort I need to know.
Copyright © 1996 Thankyou Music. Used by permission.

Alternatively, if the CD is not used, the following passage could be
read by one of the leaders at the close of their faith story.

Psalm 23

The Lord is my shepherd, I shall not be in want.
He makes me lie down in green pastures,
he leads me beside quiet waters, he restores my soul.
He guides me in paths of righteousness for his name's sake.
Even though I walk through the valley of the shadow of death,
I will fear no evil, for you are with me;
your rod and your staff, they comfort me.

You prepare a table before me in the presence of my enemies.
You anoint my head with oil; my cup overflows.
Surely goodness and love will follow me all the days of my life,
and I will dwell in the house of the Lord for ever.

Following the song or the reading, the session leader points out that
the message is a simple one: God loves us, he carries us throughout
life's journey, he is with us during both good and bad times. He
knows what we are going through. He is there to guide us on our
journey even when we feel lost. (Alternatively, John 10:1–18 could
be read at this point.)

John 10:1–18

'I tell you the truth, the man who does not enter the sheep pen by
the gate, but climbs in by some other way, is a thief and a robber.
The man who enters by the gate is the shepherd of his sheep. The
watchman opens the gate for him, and the sheep listen to his
voice. He calls his own sheep by name and leads them out. When
he has brought out all his own, he goes on ahead of them, and his
sheep follow him because they know his voice. But they will never

follow a stranger; in fact, they will run away from him because they do not recognise a stranger's voice.' Jesus used this figure of speech, but they did not understand what he was telling them.

Therefore Jesus said again, 'I tell you the truth, I am the gate for the sheep. All who ever came before me were thieves and robbers, but the sheep did not listen to them. I am the gate; whoever enters through me will be saved. He will come in and go out, and find pasture. The thief comes only to steal and kill and destroy; I have come that they may have life, and have it to the full.

'I am the good shepherd. The good shepherd lays down his life for the sheep. The hired hand is not the shepherd who owns the sheep. So when he sees the wolf coming, he abandons the sheep and runs away. Then the wolf attacks the flock and scatters it. The man runs away because he is a hired hand and cares nothing for the sheep.

'I am the good shepherd; I know my sheep and my sheep know me – just as the Father knows me and I know the Father – and I lay down my life for the sheep. I have other sheep that are not of this sheep pen . . . I lay down my life – only to take it up again. No-one takes it from me, but I lay it down of my own accord. I have authority to lay it down and authority to take it up again. This command I received from my Father.'

If this passage is used here the session leader explains that it teaches that if we listen, we can recognise God's voice and seek direction for our journey from him, even though many other voices are trying to lead us in other ways (our parents/partners, the media, teachers – to name but a few). God will guide us in the right way if we listen to his voice.

11. *Homework*

Each person keeps their pebble and is invited to bring it back the following week, changed and personalised in some way. (See homework at the end of the session.)

12. *Journey beads*

People then return to their sets. Each set leader has a jar of beads (or a variety of buttons) and places it in the centre of their group.

Members are asked to lay out their piece of string, cord or ribbon in a continuous line, symbolising a time line.

Beads or buttons are then threaded onto the piece of string and they may well correlate with the highs and lows of life, but not necessarily! Undulations are then created in the string to represent the highs and lows of life.

Leaders' Notes

During the 'journey beads' section the leader should explain that the beads can symbolise times, events or experiences that they feel were of spiritual significance to them (examples could be: a prayer at the loss of a loved one, new hope at the start of a marriage, the sadness of a divorce, a sense of God at the birth of a child, spiritual feelings of personal need when facing illness, emotions experienced on passing or failing exams).

The set leader will have to judge how long people need to do this exercise, ensuring that everyone has had enough time to complete the task. The set leader then takes leisurely feedback from their group about what the string and the beads symbolise for them.

The journey from here

13. *Conclusion to journey beads*

The session leader calls everyone back to the larger group, bringing with them their string with the beads on it. The leader explains that these experiences have made us the people we are, and that while some of our experiences may have been painful, some have enabled us to grow as people. The beads remind us that there is a spiritual dimension to our existence.

The group are invited to make their string and beads into a necklace or bracelet. During this time the leader talks through the way that everyone must effectively own their personal past.

14. *Hands*

The session closes with the meditation 'Hands', in which participants are invited to look at their hands and to release aspects of their past to God.

   Some group members may not want to clench their fists at the start of this meditation.

Hands

I see, Lord, in my tightly clenched fists a symbol of my self.
I grasp my life, hiding all I don't want others to see.
I hold my pride:
My desire to appear right, my desire to appear strong.
I hold my anxieties:
My fear that I won't be accepted as I am. My inability to be who
    I am.
I hold my anger:
My violence that protects me against anyone who comes too
    close to my secrets.
I ache with this tension, with the immense energy required to
    hide myself –
From you, lest you change me; from them, lest they hurt me.
With these fists, I want to strike out –
Against you, against them, against all that threatens me.
    [Pause]

But I see, in these whitened knuckles and straining forearms,
    what this is doing to me:
I am enslaved, imprisoned within myself. I am destroying myself
    with others. *[Pause]*
But I sense your presence, Lord, your open hands reaching out
    to me.

I slowly open my hands and release myself to you.
I offer all I have been grasping so tightly; and fear of being
    known and anxiety of being alone, the anger, the guilt, the
    pain.
Lord! My arms no longer ache! My hands can move again!
They can stretch and wiggle.
They are open and able to receive. Fill them with your love!
Show them how to touch, how to serve.

Freed from my own grasp, I am suddenly aware of others. I
    reach out to my sisters and brothers.

> *Let my hands be your hands as I take their needs and cares and lift them to you.*
> *Give us your sustaining grace, touch us with your healing love.*
> *Take us and shape us together into the body of your Son.*
> *Let our hands be your hands to reach out into the world you love.*
> Original author unknown. © Adapted by Martha Keys Barker and Patricia Beall. Celebration Services International Ltd 1973,1977.

♫ This session could be concluded with the following optional meditation improvised by Liz Babbs (track 3 on the *Essence* CD).

Palms Up, Palms Down

Sitting or lying down in a comfortable position with your palms facing the ceiling, become aware of your breathing deepening and slowing.

Now turning your palms over to face the floor, release (to God) all the things that are troubling you at the moment. You might want to imagine yourself removing a heavy back pack from your back, and unpacking all the rocks and stones that have been weighing you down.

Now turning your palms upwards again, spend a few minutes receiving God's love . . . joy . . . and peace.

Adapted by Liz Babbs from Richard Foster's book *Celebration of Discipline*. Reproduced by permission of Hodder & Stoughton.

15. *Homework*

Homework 1: Remind the group to take their pebble home and to enrich it in some way and to bring it back next week. They may, for example, polish it, paint it, wax it or stick something on it. As they enhance the pebble at home they should meditate on ways in which their own lives could become more enriched.

Homework 2: The session leader invites the group to bring to the next session three objects that are important to them and which say something about their image or identity (e.g. toy, car keys, walking boots, sports trophy, divorce papers, but NO photos). The objects they bring could be symbols of something bigger, e.g. keys for a car or a plectrum for a guitar.

Shopping list

You will need a CD player throughout this session.

Section 1

- Variety of dips (e.g. guacamole, sour cream and chives) and breads (e.g. naan, ciabatta, unleavened)

- Drinks (e.g. mineral water, fruit juice)

Section 3

- Various pieces of cord, string and ribbon, each 50 cm in length, enough for one per person

Section 7

- Scissors might be required

Section 8

- A pile of small, washed stones or pebbles – more than one each to ensure plenty of choice

Section 12

- Pile of beads of different colours, or a variety of buttons, for each small group

- One container for the beads for each group

- The string or beading cord from Section 3.

Running order – crib sheet

1. Food

2. Journey to the session

☺   3. The cord of belonging

4. Guidelines

5. Massage/touch

6. Sharing

7. Individuality

♫   8. 'Stones' meditation (meditation on CD)

9. Getting lost and being found (testimony)

♫   10. Psalm 23 (song on CD)

11. Homework

☺   12. Journey beads

13. Conclusion to journey beads

♫   14. 'Hands' (meditation) or 'Palms Up' (meditation on CD)

📖   15. Homework

The Journey Within

Key concepts: identity, image, perception, affirmation

The aim of this session is to encourage the group to consider the question 'Who am I?' The session moves through four sections: it examines what the world says about image and identity; it looks at how we view our identity; it unveils masks we hide behind; and it examines our self-image in the light of Christian teaching. The session aims to offer a sense of joy and celebration as we discover that our true identity is to be found through a fellowship with Christ.

Introduction to the journey

People arrive and are welcomed by the group leaders. The session leader explains that this session is going to look at our identity.

Leaders' Notes

It would be helpful if the leaders set out the room with open magazines and a large candle as the focus. The candle could be in the middle, with the magazines laid out on the floor at its base.

---

1. *Pebbles*

Members of the group are invited to display their pebble from the previous session and to share briefly what they did to it and why. (This activity is intended to be a brief, light-hearted one. The

interpretations don't need to be too deep or lengthy!) If the group is large, it would be better to split up into small sets for this exercise, each with its own leader.

2. *Satsumas*

The leader places a bowl of satsumas (or possibly oranges or potatoes) in the centre of the room. Everyone is invited to take a satsuma and to study the features and marks on it. The satsumas are then put back in the bowl and the leader mixes them up. Once they are mixed up everyone is invited to find their own satsuma. The session leader then explains that each and every one of us is unique and that we are all made in the image of God. People could eat their satsuma once they have found it!

How does the world see me?

3. *Identity collages*

 Everyone moves into sets (possibly same gender), each with a leader. In the centre of the room there is a large pile of magazines and newspapers. Each set is provided with tubes of glue and scissors, as well as a large piece of card in the shape of a human head and shoulders.

Leaders' Notes

Each group is given a large piece of card cut into a human shape. A line could be added across the head to symbolise the mind, and a heart shape on the chest could symbolise the heart.

(Alternatively, don't split the group up according to gender, but have a large piece of card shaped as head and shoulders and divide it into two halves, one half representing males and the other half females. This way of working could create an extra dimension for discussion in the feedback session about the male and female characteristics to be found in all of us.)

There should be a large selection of magazines, including leisure, sports, computers, women's and men's glossy monthlies and TV guides, so that everyone will find something they can use within the exercise.

This section may take up quite a lot of the session time. It is suggested that a minimum of 15 to 20 minutes be allocated.

The sets are asked to cut out pictures, images, words and phrases and to make a joint collage illustrating what societal pressures shape our aspirations for personal identity and self-image. Examples might include fashion, superstars, sex appeal, beauty, fame, cars and adverts.

As the sets carry out the task, they discuss human identity and reflect on how culture, advertising and the media influence their personal ideals of self-image. This should be a fun and entertaining activity!

4. Sharing collages

The sets gather in the larger group and a representative from each set talks through the collage that they have made in Section 3. This exercise should open up discussion on how we view ourselves, what is important to us and how we would like others to see us.

5. *Relax and be*

The session leader invites the group to share in a time of meditation and relaxation to music. The aim is to relax the body and the mind. A leader could read out the following instructions, or alternatively use the *Essence* CD, track 4.

(a) Lie back and relax, with your hands by your side, your palms facing upwards and your feet apart.

(b) Now flex your feet . . . relax [x3]
Tense your calf muscles . . . relax [x3]
Pull your thighs together . . . relax [x3]
Pull your stomach in . . . relax [x3]
Scrunch your shoulders (gently) together . . . relax [x3]
Stretch your fingers . . . relax [x3]
Stretch your arms . . . relax [x3]

(c) Counting slowly:
Breathe in deeply 2, 3, 4 . . . breathe out slowly 2, 3, 4
Breathe in peace 2, 3, 4 . . . breathe out stress 2, 3, 4

Breathe in Spirit 2, 3, 4 . . . breathe out insecurity 2, 3, 4
Breathe in love 2, 3, 4 . . . breathe out anger 2, 3, 4
Breathe in joy 2, 3, 4 . . . breathe out fear 2, 3, 4

(d) Now spend some time listening to the sounds outside the room. [Pause]
Now focus on the sounds inside the room. [Pause]
And now listen to your own breathing, trying to exclude all other sounds. [Pause]

(e) And finally relax and think about a safe place.

6. 'Who Am I?'

After an appropriate pause, the poem written by Liz Babbs is read to the group as they continue to relax as a focus to lead into the next activity.

Who Am I?

*Who am I
If I'm not famous
Not a celebrity
Don't appear in* Hello *magazine
Or in tabloid newspapers?*

*What am I worth
If I don't have lots of money
An impressive job
A flashy car
And a designer house and garden?*

*Who says I'm significant
If I'm ignored in the workplace
Taken for granted in the home
Abused by the young
And told I don't count?*

*Who am I
As I grow older*

And youth rules
Technology drives
And money speaks?

Who am I?

How do I see myself?

7. Objects

Moving back into sets, the leaders invite the participants to talk about the three objects they were asked to bring with them the week before. (The group were asked to bring objects that are important to them and which say something about their image or identity.)

Leaders' Notes

If some participants have been unable to bring three objects to the session, or if there are any new people present, the group could list their objects on a piece of paper. This section may also take quite a while, as the leaders should ensure that all participants have the opportunity to talk about their objects. The set leaders will have to keep an eye on the time during this section!

It's worth bearing in mind that some people may find this a difficult activity and may have been unable to select three objects. If this is so, it would be good to encourage them to share why they found this hard.

How can I discover the real me?

8. Masks

The group unite in a large circle and everyone is given a face-shaped paper mask with two eyeholes cut out of it. Felt-tip pens are also distributed.

The group are asked by the session leader to think about the 'masks' they hide behind in everyday life. Each participant should think about how others might perceive them, e.g. shy, out-going, kind. Get them to write these words on the outside of their mask.

The group are then invited to think about how they honestly see themselves. Ask the participants to write single words or phrases on the inside of their mask. This exercise is confidential and no one will be asked to share what they have written.

Leaders' Notes

For the 'masks' exercise, leaders should be aware that some participants might identify some sensitive and personal issues to go on the inside of their masks. It should be explained that the group will not be showing their masks to one another. If they prefer, they don't have to write on their masks at all, or their mask can be folded up and put away in a pocket as soon as this exercise is complete.

---

9. Made in God's image

This is the Christian focus of the evening. The group have already unpacked various concepts about image and identity. The thrust of the leader's testimony should be personal. It should turn the world's concepts of self-image upside down. It could be a testimony of how a personal mask was removed in the past. We believe as Christians that we are created by and made in the image of God. This is where our true identity rests.

The testimony should emphasise that God accepts us as we are, with no pretences. God does not judge us by the same standards as the world. (The collages made in Section 3 could be used here to illustrate the testimony.) God knows us inside out and we need have no pretences with him. It may be appropriate for more than one testimony to be shared.

Suggested verses to be used during this time of testimony might include:

- Psalm 139, especially verse 14: 'I praise you because I am fearfully and wonderfully made.'

- Ephesians 2:10: 'For we are God's workmanship . . .'

- 1 Timothy 4:4: 'For everything God created is good . . .'

- Genesis 1:27: 'So God created man in his own image, in the image of God he created him; male and female he created them.'

10. *Mirrors*

This optional activity involves passing mirrors around the group with verses written on them, such as Psalm 139:14: 'I praise you because I am fearfully and wonderfully made.' The verse could be painted or written on with lipstick. Several mirrors could be used for larger groups. Possible verses might include:

- Song of Songs 4:7: 'All beautiful you are, my darling; there is no flaw in you.'

- Isaiah 40:29: 'He gives strength to the weary and increases the power of the weak.'

- Isaiah 46:4: 'Even to your old age and grey hairs I am he, I am he who will sustain you. I have made you and I will carry you; I will sustain you and I will rescue you.'

- Isaiah 53:5: 'The punishment that brought us peace was upon him, and by his wounds we are healed.'

- Isaiah 57:18: 'I have seen his ways, but I will heal him; I will guide him and restore comfort to him.'

- Jeremiah 1:5: 'Before I formed you in the womb I knew you, before you were born I set you apart.'

- Jeremiah 29:11: '"For I know the plans I have for you," declares the Lord, "plans to prosper you and not to harm you, plans to give you hope and a future."'

- John 15:14: 'You are my friends if you do what I command.'

- Ephesians 2:10: 'For we are God's workmanship, created in Christ Jesus to do good works, which God prepared in advance for us to do.'

- Colossians 3:12: 'Therefore, as God's chosen people, holy and dearly loved, clothe yourselves with compassion, kindness, humility, gentleness and patience.'

The group spends a few minutes silently passing the mirrors around. As each mirror is received, the participants look at their reflection and try to apply the verse to their own life, thinking about their unique identity.

11. Candles

The leader invites the group to gather around the large church candle in the centre of the room. The leader explains that the candle represents Jesus, the Light of the World.

The participants choose a small candle from a range of tea lights on offer. They are then invited, one by one, to light their tea light candle from the larger candle in the centre. If they feel it appropriate, they may place their tea light at the foot of the large candle, as a symbol of their true identity in God.

Leaders' Notes

It should be made clear to the participants that they don't have to light their candles if they feel that it is inappropriate for them. At the close of the session the leaders could also give people the option of taking home their candle. They might want to use it during their own personal meditations or devotions while contemplating their God-given identity. (A range of different candles could be used so that participants may choose a candle they feel they associate with – maybe because of the scent or colour. This will require thought when buying the candles for the session.)

Some participants might like to place the mask they used in Section 8 underneath their lighted candle, as a further symbol that their true identity is to be found in God. It should be made clear that this action is optional.

12. *Light of the World*

To end the session, and to link in with the issues raised, the following prayer should be read out by the session leader:

Light of the World

Light of the World
infiltrate my darkness

Light of the World
restore my strength

Light of the World
illuminate my pathway

and grant me your peace
that I might find my way
home to you

© Liz Babbs

13. *Journals*

The session leader introduces the concept of journalling.

> ### Leaders' Notes
>
> Leaders could share the concept of journalling and the impor-
> tance of keeping a record of one's spiritual journey week by
> week. They should make it clear that at no point during the
> course will anyone else read these journals. See notes on jour-
> nalling at the beginning of the manual.

Participants are given the opportunity to take a small notebook home
with them. They are encouraged to note down their spiritual journey
throughout the series.

> ### Leaders' Notes
>
> Leaders should ask the group to bring to the next session any
> clean refuse and scrap materials that might be suitable for creat-
> ing models, such as cardboard tubes, egg boxes and small
> containers.

Shopping list

Section 2

• A bowl of satsumas (or oranges or potatoes) – one for each group
  member

Section 3

- A large pile of magazines and newspapers

- A large piece of card for each set

- Glue and scissors for each set

Section 7

- Paper and pens

Section 8

- Paper masks – the paper is shaped into a mask by cutting out the shape of a head and shoulders and creating two eyeholes

- Felt-tip pens for everyone

Section 10

 - A mirror (with Psalm 139:14 written on it, using either paint or lipstick), or for larger groups several mirrors with the suggested verses written on them

Section 11

- Scented or coloured tea-light candles, one for each group member

- One large church candle

Section 13

- Small notebooks to be used as journals – one for each group member

Running order – crib sheet

 1. Pebbles

2. Satsumas

 3. Identity collages

4. Sharing collages

5. Relax and be (meditation on CD)

6. 'Who Am I?'

7. Objects

8. Masks

9. Made in God's image (testimony)

10. Mirrors

11. Candles

12. Light of the World

13. Journals

The Journey to a Better World

Key concepts: a perfect creation, the eco-system, destruction, creator, stewardship, partnership

The aim of this session is to promote discussion regarding the state of the world we live in, and to face up to our personal responsibility in contributing to the destruction we see. It aims to tackle the question 'Who owns the world?' and to develop understanding of the biblical concept of stewardship. This may be a challenging session for the leaders as well as the group members!

Introduction to the journey

People arrive and are welcomed by the group leaders. The group are encouraged to share stories from their life during the previous week. Aim for a relaxed and casual atmosphere.

God's perfect world

Leaders' Notes

In preparation for the session a large cardboard jigsaw is made. On one side is a place of natural beauty and on the other a simple cross. There should be sufficient pieces for each group member to have one. The jigsaw is displayed 'Eden' side up in the centre of the room.

1. *Garden of Eden*

Everyone is invited to take one piece of the jigsaw and place it somewhere in the room while the following Bible passages are read out by a leader.

Genesis 2:1

Thus the heavens and the earth were completed in all their vast array.

Genesis 2:16–17

And the Lord God commanded the man, 'You are free to eat from any tree in the garden; but you must not eat from the tree of the knowledge of good and evil, for when you eat of it you will surely die.'

Genesis 3:1

Now the serpent was more crafty than any of the wild animals the Lord God had made. He said to the woman, 'Did God really say, "You must not eat from any tree in the garden"?'

Genesis 3:6–7

When the woman saw that the fruit of the tree was good for food and pleasing to the eye, and also desirable for gaining wisdom, she took some and ate it. She also gave some to her husband, who was with her, and he ate it. Then the eyes of both of them were opened, and they realised that they were naked; so they sewed fig leaves together and made coverings for themselves.

Our perfect world

2. *Models*

The group splits up into sets, each with a leader. In the centre of the room there is a variety of scrap materials.

Leaders' Notes

At the end of the previous session the participants were asked to bring clean pieces of refuse that could be used to create models. This scrap should be placed in the centre of the room as the group arrive and might include egg boxes, small cardboard boxes, paper tubes and coloured paper.

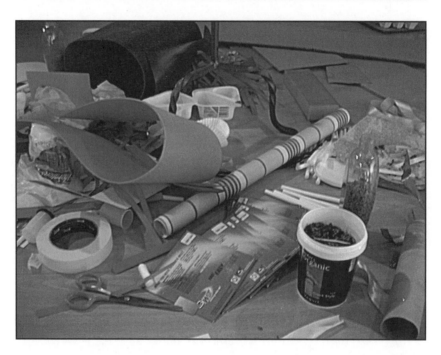

The session leader asks each set to create a model using the scrap to represent their idea of a perfect location – their image of paradise. Examples might include a desert island, a forest or a sunset. Leaders should allow at least 10 to 15 minutes for this exercise.

Leaders' Notes

Leaders should place pairs of scissors, glue and reels of tape in the centre of the room before the session begins. A limited number of such resources will mean that the sets have to share with one another. A leader could use this shortage of resources to remind the group about the need to share things globally.

3. *Relax in paradise*

The group members are invited to find a space in which to sit, kneel or lie quietly.

Leaders' Notes

A CD of natural sounds, track 5 from the *Essence* CD or soft music could be played in the background in the opening moments of this exercise. The sounds or music should be faded out once the group have had a chance to unwind and relax.

The session leader asks the group to imagine that they are in a perfect place. This could be an imaginary place or one that is real. The session leader helps the group to explore their imaginary scene by posing helpful questions. For example: What can you see? What can you hear? What can you see on the horizon? What colour is the sky? Are there any clouds? Stretch out your hands. What can you feel? Is it warm or cold?

When the session leader has finished guiding the group in this way, the participants should be encouraged to 'live and enjoy' their paradise for a few minutes!

After this the leader encourages participants to describe their dream location to the person next to them.

4. *The world*

The group is split up into sets, each with its own leader. Newspapers are spread out to protect the floor. A large inflatable globe, a beach ball or an A2 map of the world is given to each set, along with some brightly coloured thick marker pens.

Leaders' Notes

Some large post-it notes could be used instead of marker pens. They may be more appropriate if you are using an inflatable globe and you want to reuse it afterwards.

The sets are encouraged to think about how, as human beings, we have damaged the world. Using the marker pens the sets graffiti their 'world' using words or symbols. Ask them to be specific about ecological issues, for example greed, globalisation, vandalism, litter, pollution, waste, gas emissions, war, hate, abuse, hunger and industrialisation.

5. *'How We Break the World!'*

Keeping the focus on the graffitied map/globe, the meditation 'How We Break the World!' is read by a leader or played from the *Essence* CD, track 6.

How We Break the World!

The first commandment is:
'Love the Lord your God
with all your heart,
soul, mind and strength.'
But we don't. . . .

We ignore our Creator.
We break the world.
We love our possessions.
We explain all things without God.

We are strong enough to destroy the planet!
We have broken our promises
We have broken the world
We are breaking our Father's heart,
And yet he loves.
For God so loved the world
that he gave his only Son,
Jesus Christ.
The Lord our God can give new life.
He restores my soul.

We see his healing hands at work in all creation.
We hear his call to turn to him
and start again.

© Rob Frost

6. Owning up to responsibility

The music continues. As a way of reflecting on our responsibility for what the world has become, the group are invited to get their hands dirty!

A tray of water-based children's paint (ideally red) is handed out to each set. Participants dip a finger into the paint and place finger-prints over the 'graffiti' on the globe. This is an admission of per-sonal responsibility for the part we have played in damaging the world. Even though this is a fun activity it can also be done in a deadly serious manner.

The sets are encouraged to think about how, as human beings, we could heal the world. Using the marker pens already provided, the sets redeem their 'world' using positive words or symbols. Ask the sets to identify specific ways in which they could make a positive contribution to ecology, for example recycling schemes, using public transport, taking part in local conservation activities, using less energy, buying organic/fair-trade products.

The set leader then encourages participants to write on their map/globe their personal contributions to helping the world. For each personal promise made, the participants are encouraged to place a green fingerprint over the words as a symbol of their commitment. A tray of green paint is provided for this purpose.

Leaders' Notes

Leaders should have a bucket of water and a towel ready for each set to clean their fingers after the finger-paint exercise. The use of children's water-based paint will mean that it can be removed from hands and clothes easily! Remember that the floor should be covered by newspaper or bin liners to protect it.

7. *String web*

The whole group is invited to stand in a large circle. The leader holds the end of a large ball of wool or string and throws the ball to another participant. This is repeated until each member is holding onto the string. In this way a web is formed. This activity illustrates the intricate connection of us all to the fragile eco-system. Once the web has been constructed the group try to bounce the globe on top of it!

Leaders' Notes

Leaders need to make sure that all of the participants are included in the web. Once the web is complete it may be relevant for someone to talk briefly about the environment and the future prospects of our eco-system. This person should have been briefed beforehand. It does not have to be a leader but could be someone in the group who is both knowledgeable and passionate about these issues.

The session leader then asks a couple of people in the circle to let go of their section of the web. Gradually, as more and more participants let go, the web becomes weak and misshapen, thus illustrating the importance of our individual responsibility in contributing towards the well being of the earth. The group place the web on the floor and sit down in a circle.

Whose world is it anyway?

8. Whose world?

 Working in sets, each set is given one of the following Bible passages written on card. The sets are asked to discuss what their Bible passage teaches about the concept of a Creator. Do they agree or disagree?

- Genesis 1:20–21: 'And God said, "Let the water teem with living creatures, and let birds fly above the earth across the expanse of the sky." So God created the great creatures of the sea and every living and moving thing with which the water teems, according to their kinds, and every winged bird according to its kind. And God saw that it was good.'

- Genesis 1:26–27: 'Then God said, "Let us make man in our image, in our likeness, and let them rule over the fish of the sea and the birds of the air, over the livestock, over all the earth, and over all the creatures that move along the ground." So God created man in his own image, in the image of God he created him; male and female he created them.'

- Genesis 2:4–7: 'This is the account of the heavens and the earth when they were created. When the Lord God made the earth and the heavens – and no shrub of the field had yet appeared on the earth and no plant of the field had yet sprung up, for the Lord God had not sent rain on the earth and there was no man to work the ground, but streams came up from the earth and watered the whole surface of the ground – the Lord God formed the man from the dust of the ground and breathed into his nostrils the breath of life, and the man became a living being.'

- Psalm 145:9: 'The Lord is good to all; he has compassion on all he has made.'

- Psalm 147:4: 'He determines the number of the stars and calls them each by name.'

- Psalm 24:1–2: 'The earth is the Lord's, and everything in it, the world, and all who live in it; for he founded it upon the seas and established it upon the waters.'

The leader explains that the Creator needs a community of people whose spirituality calls them to be good stewards over creation and to work in partnership with him. One of the leaders could give a testimony at this point. They could talk about Christ's redemption in their own life and how their personal renewal has given them a greater sense of responsibility for the created order. They could explain that we have no rights over the world, but are called to be stewards of it before God.

9. *Prayer: 'My Dear King'*

The leader invites the group to listen to a ninth-century prayer.

My Dear King

*My dear king. My own king, without pride, without sin, you
    created the whole world.*
*You existed before the elements, before the sun was set in the
    sky,*
Before the waters covered the ocean floor;
Beautiful king, you are without beginning and without end.

You created the land out of shapeless mass,
You carved the mountains and chiselled the valleys
And covered the earth with trees and grass.
*You measured each object and each span within the
    universe:*
The heights of the mountains
And the depths of the oceans:
The distance from the sun to the moon
And from star to star.
And you created men and women
To be your stewards of the earth
Always praising you, for you are boundless love.

The work of redemption

10. *Jigsaw*

Everyone is invited to find the pieces of the jigsaw spread around the room at the beginning of the session, and to place them together in the centre of the room, with the 'Garden of Eden' side down and the cross revealed. Once this is done, a leader reads out John 3:16–17.

John 3:16–17

For God so loved the world that he gave his one and only Son, that whoever believes in him shall not perish but have eternal life. For God did not send his Son into the world to condemn the world, but to save the world through him.

The leader then speaks about the cross and God's redeeming work in the world. By receiving the love of Jesus expressed through his sacrifice made on the cross, we discover his redeeming work in our lives and become a part of the people who are reclaiming the world in his name. The group moves into a relaxed position and the leader reads out the verses below.

Romans 6:21

But now that you've found you don't have to listen to sin tell you what to do, and have discovered the delight of listening to God telling you, what a surprise! A whole, healed, put-together life right now, with more and more of life on the way! Work hard for sin your whole life and your pension is death. But God's gift is real life, eternal life, delivered by Jesus, our Master.

(The Message)

Romans 8:19–23

That's why I don't think there's any comparison between the present hard times and the coming good times. The created world itself can hardly wait for what's coming next. Everything in creation is being more or less held back. God reins it in until both creation and all the creatures are ready and can be released at the same moment into the glorious times ahead. Meanwhile, the joyful anticipation deepens.

All around us we observe a pregnant creation. The difficult times of pain throughout the world are simply birth pangs . . . These sterile and barren bodies of ours are yearning for full deliverance. That is why waiting does not diminish us, any more than waiting diminishes a pregnant mother. We are enlarged in the waiting. We, of course, don't see what is enlarging us. But the longer we wait, the larger we become, and the more joyful our expectancy.

(The Message)

After the verses have been read out, there are a few moments of silence. Quiet music is then played while another leader reads out the poem 'I See His blood upon the Rose'.

I See His Blood upon the Rose

I see His blood upon the rose
And in the stars the glory of His eyes,
His body gleams amid eternal snows,
His tears fall from the skies.

I see His face in every flower;
The thunder and the singing of the birds
Are but His voice – and carven by His power
Rocks are His written words.

All pathways by His feet are worn,
His strong heart stirs the ever-beating sea,
His crown of thorns is twisted in every thorn,
His cross is every tree.

Joseph Mary Plunkett (1887–1916)

11. *Bless the world*

The group stands and forms a circle, and the session leader asks the group to slowly pass a globe (or ball representing the world) from one to another. As each individual takes the globe they say the name of a country. The session leader ends by saying a short prayer asking God to bless all these countries. The leader reminds the group that we are stewards of creation until the end of time – when Christians believe that God will make the redemption of the world complete.

The session ends with the leader reading this passage from Revelation about the new heaven and the new earth. The leader explains that this passage encourages Christians to work towards the day when Jesus will be seen at the heart of the new creation.

Revelation 21:1–4

Then I saw a new heaven and a new earth, for the first heaven and the first earth had passed away, and there was no longer any sea. I saw the Holy City, the new Jerusalem, coming down out of heaven from God, prepared as a bride beautifully dressed for her husband. And I heard a loud voice from the throne saying, 'Now the dwelling of God is with men, and he will live with them. They will be his people, and God himself will be with them and be their God. He will wipe every tear from their eyes. There will be no more death or mourning or crying or pain, for the old order of things has passed away.'

This reading should be followed by a time of silence (suggested two minutes) to give the group members a chance to reflect on what they have learned and shared.

Shopping list

Section 1

- A large piece of card made into a jigsaw – a picture of natural beauty on one side and a picture of a cross on the other

Section 3

- A CD of natural sounds or soft music, or the *Essence* CD

Section 4

- Large inflatable globe, beach ball or similar, or A2 map of the world (one for each set)

- Brightly coloured marker pens

- Old newspapers

- Large post-it notes

Section 6

- Water-based children's paint (red and green)

- Paint tray or paper plates

- Old newspapers or bin liners

- Soap, bowl of water and a towel

- Large post-it notes (a different colour from those used in Section 4)

Section 7

- Ball•of wool or string

- A blow-up globe or ball

Section 8

- Pieces of card

Section 11

- A globe or ball

Running order – crib sheet

1. Garden of Eden
☺ 2. Models
♫ 3. Relax in paradise (music on CD)
☺ 4. The World
♫ 5. 'How we break the world!' (meditation on CD)
☺ 6. Owning up to responsibility
   7. String web
☺ 8. Whose world?
   9. Prayer: 'My dear King'
10. Jigsaw
11. Bless the world

The Journey to Wholeness

Key concepts: body, mind, spirit, emotions, physical and mental pain

In this session we examine the experience of physical, emotional and mental pain and how all three are connected. We look at the spiritual dimension behind these concepts, and discuss wholeness and how it can be discovered through God's healing power. We examine what it means to be healed by God, and what form such healing might take.

Introduction to the journey

People arrive and are welcomed by the leaders.

1. *Yellow dough*

With relaxing music playing in the background the session leader asks the group to form a large circle. A large lump of yellow salt dough or play dough is handed round the group. (See dough recipes at the end of the session.)

Everyone is asked to take a piece of the dough as it is handed around. Individuals then form the dough into shapes that symbolise happy times in their lives. Examples might include a holiday, a wedding, passing exams.

Leaders' Notes

Leaders will have to keep watch on the time as some may want to take too long creating something elaborate.

Once the group have had an opportunity to form their shapes in the dough, they are asked to place their shapes on a tray in the centre of the room.

Journey through the pain

2. Types of pain

The group stay in a circle. The session leader gives each person a large nail to hold and then introduces the subject of pain, using examples of different types of pain – emotional, physical and mental. The leader may describe their own experiences of different types of pain to introduce this section.

Leaders' Notes

This introduction to different types of pain should be kept short and to the point.

The participants are invited to press the nail lightly into the palm of their hand. They are asked to think of times in their lives when they have experienced different types of pain. The group should not be rushed. Allow two or three minutes for individuals to reflect on painful times.

 The meditation 'Renew Me Lord' by Liz Babbs is read out or played from the *Essence* CD, track 7.

Renew Me Lord

And bring Your healing and forgiveness.

Refresh me Lord
And bring life into the staleness of my existence
Fresh hope in disillusionment

Release me Lord from this numbing pain
And help me to feel the warmth
Of Your love again
(Taken from the book *Out of the Depths*, p. 32,
by Liz Babbs © Eagle 2001)

3. *Red dough*

After the meditation is finished, the group splits up into sets, each with a leader. Everyone takes their nail with them.

☺   A large ball of red salt dough or play dough is passed around the sets and everyone is invited to take a piece.

The session leader invites the group to shape the dough in some way to symbolise difficult experiences in their lives, and some kind of pain they have experienced (e.g. physical suffering, mental anguish). They are asked to use their nail as part of their symbol (if they wish to do so), or to use the nail to shape the dough in some way. This activity is done in silence.

Once the sets have completed their symbols, the leader encourages the participants to share what they have made (if they are happy to do so).

Leaders' Notes

It should be emphasised that there is no pressure for people to talk about their symbols at this point if they do not wish to do so.

Following this, the questions below could be used to trigger conversation about the pain individuals have known:

- Which is worse – physical, emotional or mental pain?

- When did you last cry?

- How are the experiences of pain in body, mind and spirit connected (e.g. toothache can make us feel under the weather generally)?

- Can spiritual lows affect us physically?

Once the conversation has finished, individuals should place their dough models on the tray alongside their other dough models.

Moving towards wholeness

4. *Wholeness in God*

The sets move back into a large group and form a circle. The group leader explains that during this next section we will be looking at wholeness, and what it means to be a whole person. The leader introduces the Christian principle of body, mind and spirit fully integrated by God's love in our lives, and explains that God, our Creator, is the one who has the power to enable us to become whole and integrated people.

It should be explained that becoming whole may not necessarily bring about quick or easy resolutions to our problems. It can take a long time to move to the perfect wholeness God wants for us.

To illustrate this, leaders share testimony about how God has used painful or dark experiences in their own lives to enrich them or to teach them more about his purposes.

Leaders' Notes

This section should communicate that God is always with us, even in dark and painful times in our lives. It would be good to have testimony from two or three Christians in the group who have come through difficult periods in their lives, and who have found a growing sense of wholeness in God.

The following passage can be used as an example of how God brings wholeness:

Mark 10:46–52

Then they came to Jericho. As Jesus and his disciples, together with a large crowd, were leaving the city, a blind man, Bartimaeus (that is, the Son of Timaeus), was sitting by the roadside begging. When he heard that it was Jesus of Nazareth, he began to shout, 'Jesus, Son of David, have mercy on me!'

Many rebuked him and told him to be quiet, but he shouted all the more, 'Son of David, have mercy on me!'

Jesus stopped and said, 'Call him.'

So they called to the blind man, 'Cheer up! On your feet! He's calling you.' Throwing his cloak aside, he jumped to his feet and came to Jesus.

'What do you want me to do for you?' Jesus asked him.

The blind man said, 'Rabbi, I want to see.'

'Go,' said Jesus, 'your faith has healed you.' Immediately he received his sight and followed Jesus along the road.

The leader explains that Bartimaeus had to tell Jesus what he wanted before Jesus could heal him. The leader gives testimony of how they have asked God to move in their own life, and how God has answered prayer.

Leaders' Notes

A testimony of healing could also be used here, but we should be aware that healing doesn't just come in our physical body. There can be a healing of the mind, emotions or spirit too.

We should not assume that people always want to be healed. Furthermore, there are many faithful Christians who are waiting for their physical healing to be completed, but have already found a sense of spiritual wholeness in God.

The session leader asks the group to find a space in which to stretch out and relax. He or she then asks the following question and invites them to reflect on it: 'What would you like to ask God to do for you today?' A couple of moments' silence follow.

As the group quietly contemplate this question, the track 'The gentle healer' by Michael Card (track 8 on the *Essence* CD) should be played.

5. *Tiles*

Once the track has finished, the session leader asks everyone to move back into their sets.

Leaders' Notes

The floor space that each group is using will have to be protected with newspaper or bin liners. It is also recommended that eye protection be used during this activity. Soft music could be playing quietly in the background throughout.

A sack or bag full of old coloured crockery/tiles is given to each set and placed in a plastic container, such as a washing-up bowl. A hammer and protective goggles are also provided.

The leader asks the participants to take it in turns to 'carefully' smash up the crockery/tiles in their sacks inside the containers.

After the crockery/tiles are smashed into small pieces (approximately 2 cm square), the broken pieces are poured into the plastic container. As this is done, the set leader initiates conversation about brokenness and how spiritual, emotional and mental suffering causes brokenness in our lives.

Recreated whole

6. *Mosaic*

 Each set is then given a 'ready to use' Polyfilla-type paste and a wood, hardboard or thick cardboard base approximately 50 × 30 cm in size. The groups are encouraged to create a beautiful mosaic on the board, maybe containing a pattern or a picture. The sets may want to discuss the shape of this before embarking on the task!

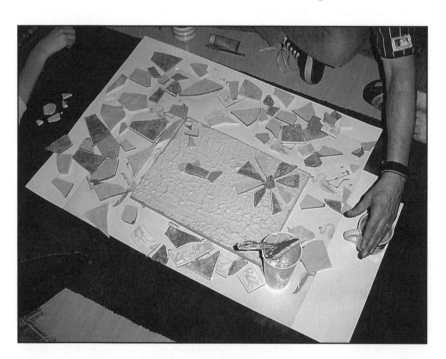

During this exercise the set leaders initiate a conversation about healing. The following questions may be used as a starter:

• Have you ever had a personal experience of healing?

- Is healing always a physical experience?

- Can we be whole and yet not physically healthy?

- Can God heal people today?

- Would you like God to heal you of a specific emotional, physical or spiritual problem?

7. 'Such Love'

The sets return to the larger group. The session leader asks a representative from each set to talk about the mosaic pattern or picture they have created.

See notes on feedback in the guidelines on page 15.

If appropriate, the group members could move into a relaxed position, and Liz Babbs' meditation/prayer 'Such Love' (track 9 on the *Essence* CD) could be played, giving the opportunity for the group to reflect on the issues raised during the session so far.

8. *Potter and clay*

The session leader explains how the healing ministry of Jesus is motivated by love and Jesus still wants to heal today. We must be aware that God's healing may take many different forms and occur over differing lengths of time.

Refer back to Leaders' Notes in Section 4 of this session.

The following reading about the potter and the clay is to be read out by one of the leaders and used as an example of how we need to give God room to move within our lives. We need to let him form us and shape us.

Jeremiah 18:1–6

This is the word that came to Jeremiah from the Lord: 'Go down to the potter's house, and there I will give you my message.' So I went down to the potter's house, and I saw him working at the wheel. But the pot he was shaping from the clay was marred in his hands; so the potter formed it into another pot, shaping it as seemed best to him.

Then the word of the Lord came to me: 'O house of Israel, can I not do with you as this potter does?' declares the Lord. 'Like clay in the hand of the potter, so are you in my hand, O house of Israel.'

9. Dough creations

The leader invites the group to take their dough shapes made earlier in the session and to shape them into something new, illustrating transformation or redemption (but only if they wish to do this). They should mix together the yellow and the red dough shapes to symbolise that painful experiences are as important in our personal development as happy ones.

During this silent activity the group members may want to ask Jesus for his help in their personal healing. The session leader invites the participants to share openly about what they have created and why, if they wish to do so. There is to be no pressure to share anything!

Leaders' Notes

The dough mixed together will form different shades of red and yellow, depending on how much dough was used for the happy and painful creations.

---

10. *Make me a channel*

To round off this session on wholeness, the ancient prayer 'Instrument of Your Peace' could be read out by a leader. Alternatively, the song 'Make me a channel of Your peace' could be sung by several members of the group.

Instrument of Your Peace

Lord, make me an instrument of your peace.
Where there is hatred, let me sow love,
Where there is injury, pardon,
Where there is doubt, faith,
Where there is despair, hope,
Where there is darkness, light,
Where there is sadness, joy.
O Divine Master, grant that I may not so much seek to be
  consoled as to console,
not so much to be understood as to understand,
not so much to be loved, as to love;
for it is in giving that we receive,
it is in pardoning that we are pardoned,
it is in dying that we awake to eternal life.
                    Author unknown, associated with St Francis of Assisi

Make Me a Channel of Your Peace

Make me a channel of Your peace.
Where there is hatred let me bring Your love;
Where there is injury, Your pardon, Lord;
And where there's doubt, true faith in You.

Chorus:
    Oh, Master, grant that I may never seek
    So much to be consoled as to console;
    To be understood as to understand;
    To be loved as to love with all my soul.

Make me a channel of Your peace.
Where there's despair in life let me bring hope;
Where there is darkness, only light;
And where there's sadness, ever joy.

Make me a channel of Your peace.
It is in pardoning that we are pardoned,
In giving to all men that we receive,
And in dying that we're born to eternal life.

Sebasian Temple © Franciscan
Communications 1967

11. *Prayer*

The group move together and sit in a circle, with everyone placing their left hand on the right shoulder of the person next to them. Once a full circle has been formed the leader prays a simple prayer for the emotional, spiritual and physical wholeness of the group. This ends with a time of silence (suggested length: two minutes).

At the end of this session it may be appropriate in some groups for the leader to pray for individuals who specially request this to help them in their ongoing search for wholeness.

Leaders' Notes

The group should be consulted before this final activity is started. Only continue with it if everyone is in agreement.

Shopping list

Section 1

- Yellow play dough or salt dough, enough for everyone in the group. (This can be purchased from a toyshop or made using the recipe below.)

- Trays

Section 2

- A large nail for each person

Section 3

- Red play dough or salt dough, enough for everyone in the group. (This can be purchased from a toyshop or made using the recipe below.)

Section 5

- Old crockery/tiles (enough for a pile for each group)

- A plastic bag or an old pillowcase, and a large plastic box or bowl for each set

- A hammer for each set

- Old newspapers/black bin liners/plastic sheeting

- Protective goggles (can be purchased from a DIY store) for each set

Section 6

- Ready made Polyfilla, one tub/tube for each set

- A wood or hardboard base (approx. 50×30 cm) for each set

Running order – crib sheet

    1. Yellow dough

♫   2. Types of pain (meditation on CD)

☺   3. Red dough

♫   4. Wholeness in God (song on CD)

☺   5. Tiles

☺   6. Mosaic

♫   7. 'Such Love' (meditation on CD)

    8. Potter and clay

    9. Dough creations

▶ 10. Make me a channel

  11. Prayer

Leaders' Notes

Leaders should be aware that difficult issues could be raised during this session on wholeness. They should only offer counselling if they are trained and qualified to do so. Those who are not trained to give counselling can still provide a listening ear and pray with people. The Association of Christian Counsellors might be a good starting point if a member of the group seeks further counselling.

The Association of Christian Counsellors
173a Wokingham Road
Reading RG6 1LT

Tel: 0118 966 2207
Fax: 0118 926 9635
Email: christian.counsel@zetnet.co.uk

Recipe for Salt Dough

Makes enough for 6–8 people.

2 cups of plain flour
1 cup of salt
1½ cups of water
A couple of drops of glycerin
Food colouring – red or yellow

1. Place all ingredients into a bowl.
2. Knead until a dough is formed.

To keep the salt-dough models, cook on a very low heat for approximately two hours, or until hard. (The length of time needed in the oven will depend on the thickness of the shapes made.)

Recipe for Play Dough

Makes enough for 6–8 people.

2 cups of plain flour
1 cup of salt
1½ cups of water
2 tbs food colouring – yellow or red
2 tbs cooking oil
2 tsp cream of tartar

1. Place all ingredients in a saucepan over a medium heat.
2. Stir until the ingredients become a solid ball.
3. Knead.
4. Store in an airtight container and keep in the fridge until required.

The Journey to Spirituality

Key concepts: spirituality, religious experience, seeking God, types of prayer, coming into God's presence

The aim of this session is to encourage the group to examine what it means to practise the presence of God. We will examine 'religious' or 'spiritual' experience in the light of Christian teaching.

Introduction to the journey

Members of the group arrive and are made welcome by the leaders. There should be a relaxed and casual atmosphere. As the group comes together, a time of sharing news from the previous week should follow.

Our relationship with God

1. *Pass the parcel*

The group comes together and sits in a large circle. The session leader introduces a gift-wrapped present and tells the group that they are going to play pass the parcel, but with a difference! The leader explains that there is a new rule: the present is *not* to be unwrapped as the music stops, but is simply to be passed on to the next person. After a few 'goes' around the circle the present is placed in the centre of the room. The session leader does not elaborate on the reason for this, but simply says, 'Sometimes in life we just let the good things and the God things pass us by.'

Leaders' Notes

It is suggested that the parcel be a luxurious box of chocolates, which is gift-wrapped to disguise it. The chocolates will be unwrapped at the end of the session and will be used as an illustration of unwrapping the good things and the God things in our lives. Background music for pass the parcel could be the latest chart music.

2. *Pictures*

The leader invites the group each to draw a picture that illustrates their relationship with God. Paper and a selection of felt-tip pens, crayons and coloured pencils should be made available for this.

Leaders' Notes

Leaders should not give examples to help the group with this exercise! The participants should be given the time and space to

> think about their picture for themselves. The exercise should make them think about how they perceive God and help them to explore their relationship with him.

Once the participants have had the opportunity to complete their pictures, the session leader invites them to move into sets and, if they wish, to share their drawings and the meanings behind them.

Leaders' Notes

There should be no pressure for the participants to share their pictures if they do not wish to.

3. *Word pictures of God*

The purpose of this exercise is to help the group to understand more about their spiritual experience. The leaders introduce three different spiritual experiences, listed below in examples (a), (b) and (c). Excerpts could be read out or paraphrased by different leaders.

Leaders' Notes

Leaders could take this opportunity to explain that Christian spiritual experiences can take many different shapes and forms.

(a) Theodore Roosevelt

He was one of the most powerful men in the world, and used to explore the 'beyond', in an exercise he called cutting himself down to size.

'Theodore and I used to play a little game together. After an evening of talk, we would go out onto the lawn and search the skies until we found the faint spot of light-mist beyond the lower

left-hand corner of the Great Square of Pegasus. Then one or the other of us would recite: "That is the spiral galaxy in Andromeda. It is as large as our Milky Way. It is one of a hundred million galaxies. It consists of one hundred million suns, each larger than our sun." Then Roosevelt would grin at me and say: "Now I think we are small enough! Let's go to bed."'

© William Beebe, *The Book of Naturalists*,
Princeton University Press, 1988

(b) Isaiah 6:1–9 – Isaiah's Commission

In the year that King Uzziah died, I saw the Lord seated on a throne, high and exalted, and the train of his robe filled the temple. Above him were seraphs, each with six wings: With two wings they covered their faces, with two they covered their feet, and with two they were flying. And they were calling to one another: 'Holy, holy, holy is the Lord Almighty; the whole earth is full of his glory.' At the sound of their voices the doorposts and thresholds shook and the temple was filled with smoke.

'Woe to me!' I cried. 'I am ruined! For I am a man of unclean lips, and I live among a people of unclean lips, and my eyes have seen the King, the Lord Almighty.'

Then one of the seraphs flew to me with a live coal in his hand, which he had taken with tongs from the altar. With it he touched my mouth and said, 'See, this has touched your lips; your guilt is taken away and your sin atoned for.'

Then I heard the voice of the Lord saying, 'Whom shall I send? And who will go for us?'

And I said, 'Here am I. Send me!'

He said, 'Go and tell this people: "Be ever hearing, but never understanding; be ever seeing, but never perceiving."'

(c) Revelation 1:12–18 – John's Picture of God

I turned round to see the voice that was speaking to me. And when I turned I saw seven golden lampstands, and among the lampstands was someone 'like a son of man', dressed in a robe reaching down to his feet and with a golden sash round his chest. His head and hair were white like wool, as white as snow, and his eyes were like blazing fire. His feet were like bronze glowing in a furnace, and his voice was like the sound of rushing waters. In his right hand he held seven stars, and out of his mouth came a sharp double-edged sword. His face was like the sun shining in all its brilliance.

When I saw him, I fell at his feet as though dead. Then he placed his right hand on me and said: 'Do not be afraid. I am the First and the Last. I am the Living One; I was dead, and behold I am alive for ever and ever! And I hold the keys of death and Hades . . .'

What is a spiritual experience?

4. *Spiritual experiences*

Moving back into sets, each with a leader, participants are invited to share spiritual experiences (both good and bad) that they may have had in the past. Examples might include dreams, sensing the closeness of God at significant places or times, a view from a mountain top, healings, giving birth, seeing God's power through nature, sunsets, the night sky.

The session leader could conclude the discussion about spiritual experience by explaining that, for Christians, spiritual experience is about coming into an awareness of the reality of God, through his Son Jesus Christ.

5. *Weaving*

This activity follows on from the previous discussion. It will give participants the opportunity to bring different spiritual experiences together in a way that will value each one individually.

Leaders' Notes

If your group is large, this activity will work better in smaller sets. It would be useful if the group could be shown a 'weave' that had been made earlier. This would enable them to grasp the weaving concept more easily.

The leader invites the sets to work on the floor in the following way. One participant takes a strip of card and lays it on the floor saying, 'This represents the time when . . .' (They then share an experience that has felt in some way 'spiritual' to them, for example a sunset, the birth of a baby, falling in love, an answer to prayer.)

A second person takes a strip of a different colour and lays it across the first, saying something similar. Participants then follow on, as they wish to, taking different coloured cards and laying them across the strips already laid. The group are encouraged to interweave the strips so that a colour pattern is formed.

As the pattern develops, the leader encourages the group to see that the diversity of our experiences helps us to recognise that we are all different and that we all encounter 'spiritual' things in different ways.

The leader explains that the Bible portrays a colourful pattern of different spiritual experiences, for example Moses (burning bush), Elijah (still small voice), the disciples at Pentecost (tongues of fire).

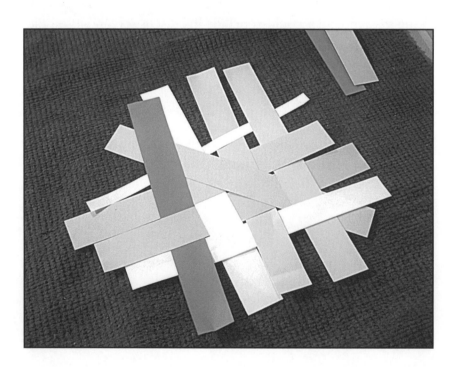

Christian experiences

6. *My story*

Participants return to the main group and two leaders share testimony of their experience of coming into a relationship with Jesus. The testimony should make it clear that their relationship continues and that this is central to their lives. Each testimony should describe how Christian experience has enriched them.

> ### Leaders' Notes
>
> This section is probably the most crucial aspect of the series, as the leaders, and possibly other Christians, share their own experience of Christian spirituality and how it has worked for them.

7. *The Prodigal Son*

Jesus illustrated his teaching by telling stories. One of the most famous of these stories is The Prodigal Son. This story shows something of God's longing for a living relationship with each of us.

The group are asked to listen to the story of the Prodigal Son on the *Essence* CD and while doing so to decide which of these main characters they identify with most (the father, the younger son or the older son).

> ### Leaders' Notes
>
> The *Essence* CD has two versions of the story of the Prodigal Son, both written by Rob Lacey (tracks 10 and 11). Leaders will have to decide before the session which version they would like to use and which is most suited to their group.

The stories on the *Essence* CD are updated versions of the parable of the Prodigal Son, based on Luke 15:11–32. Some groups may prefer to use the straight Bible reading, given here.

Luke 15:11–32 – The Prodigal Son

Jesus continued: 'There was a man who had two sons. The younger one said to his father, "Father, give me my share of the estate." So he divided his property between them.

'Not long after that, the younger son got together all he had, set off for a distant country and there squandered his wealth in wild living. After he had spent everything, there was a severe famine in that whole country, and he began to be in need. So he went and hired himself out to a citizen of that country, who sent him to his fields to feed pigs. He longed to fill his stomach with the pods that the pigs were eating, but no-one gave him anything.

'When he came to his senses, he said, "How many of my father's hired men have food to spare, and here I am starving to death! I will set out and go back to my father and say to him: Father, I have sinned against heaven and against you. I am no longer worthy to be called your son; make me like one of your hired men." So he got up and went to his father.

'But while he was still a long way off, his father saw him and was filled with compassion for him; he ran to his son, threw his arms around him and kissed him.

'The son said to him, "Father, I have sinned against heaven and against you. I am no longer worthy to be called your son."

'But the father said to his servants, "Quick! Bring the best robe and put it on him. Put a ring on his finger and sandals on his feet. Bring the fattened calf and kill it. Let's have a feast and celebrate. For this son of mine was dead and is alive again; he was lost and is found." So they began to celebrate.

'Meanwhile, the older son was in the field. When he came near the house, he heard music and dancing. So he called one of the servants and asked him what was going on. "Your brother has come," he replied, "and your father has killed the fattened calf because he has him back safe and sound."

'The older brother became angry and refused to go in. So his father went out and pleaded with him. But he answered his father, "Look! All these years I've been slaving for you and never dis-

obeyed your orders. Yet you never gave me even a young goat so I could celebrate with my friends. But when this son of yours who has squandered your property with prostitutes comes home, you kill the fattened calf for him!"

"'My son," the father said, "you are always with me, and everything I have is yours. But we had to celebrate and be glad, because this brother of yours was dead and is alive again; he was lost and is found."'

8. *Role plays*

When the story has finished the session leader asks the participants to spend a couple of minutes thinking about the character they identified with most.

The participants then divide into three character sub-groups: the fathers, the older brothers, and the younger brothers. Paper and pens are made available to each group.

These sub-groups are asked to work in role, imagining themselves into the feelings of their chosen character. Each group is asked to work out six to eight questions they would like to ask the other two characters. For example, the older brother might ask the younger brother what right he thought he had to come back home.

In turn, the groups put their questions to the corresponding groups. Each group replies to the questions in role as best they can.

Leaders' Notes

The leader may need to guide this discussion and make sure that the different character groups are not talking at the same time!

9. *Exploration of the Prodigal*

The leader explains that the group are going to explore the story of the Prodigal more deeply. This will take the form of an extended Ignatian-style meditation. Participants are led to experience the story further by seeing things through the eyes of different characters.

> **Leaders' Notes**
>
> For background information on leading Ignatian forms of meditation, see Leaders' Guidelines: Sessions, p. 17.

🎵 The following meditation can be played from the *Essence* CD, track 12, or read out by a leader.

The Prodigal Son

Imagine that you have become a part of the scene that you've just heard described (Luke 15:11–32) and that you are now the rebellious Prodigal Son. How does that feel? How do you feel about your father? What does he look like? How old is he? Is he gentle or stern? What is he wearing? What are you wearing? [Pause]

What does your older brother look like? How much older is he than you? Is he your father's favourite or are you? How do you feel about him? [Pause]

Now imagine yourself saying to your father, 'I want my share of your money and I want it now!' How do you feel – are you angry, or simply ecstatic? What do you think your father is thinking and feeling? [Pause] *Imagine yourself turning your back on your family now for ever. How does that feel? Is it painful or a relief to say goodbye?* [Pause]

Visualise this new country that you are entering, where the rich and famous 'hang out'. What does it look like? What sounds or music can you hear? Who are your new friends now? What do they do all day and all night? [Pause] *What do you do?* [Pause] *Do you think your new friends like you, or your money?* [5-second pause]

Now enjoy the excitement of being free at last, free to live the celebrity lifestyle you've always dreamed of. Free to do exactly what you want, when you want – to live a life of excess: wildly, selfishly, extravagantly. [10-second pause]

Your money has now run out. What does it feel like to be with the rich and famous and not even have enough money for a round of drinks? [Pause] *Where are your friends now? How do they treat you? Who cares about you? How does it feel to be totally alone in a foreign land – to be irrelevant, to be ignored? Feel the pain of that loneliness now. How does it feel to be starving . . . to be dirty . . . to be humiliated . . . to be reduced to working with pigs and not even be offered their food?* [15-second pause]

Now imagine yourself turning your back on this lifestyle that promised so much but delivered so little. How does it feel to know that you've failed . . . to feel defeated, empty and worthless . . . to be totally desperate? [15-second pause] *Now think about your homeland again. Even your father's employees are treated better than you've been. Do you think your father might take you back if you worked as one of his labourers?* [Pause]

Now imagine the long exhausting journey home. [Long pause] *Are you worried about seeing your father again? What are you going to say to him if he will see you?* [12-second pause]

Now catch sight of your father in the distance. [Pause] *He's running towards you, with his arms outstretched. This is more than you could ever have hoped for, more than you deserve. You're lost for words as you feel the warmth and tenderness of his embrace. How are you feeling now?* [5-second pause] *Hear yourself saying, 'Father, I've really messed up. I don't even deserve to be called your son any more.' But your father is so overjoyed that he's already organising the most lavish of parties in your honour.* [Pause]

Your brother, meanwhile, is angry and jealous at the way you're being treated, considering how you've behaved. And he's planning to boycott the party. How do you feel about your brother now? [Pause] *Your father pleads with your brother, 'My son, you are always with me, and everything I have is yours. But we have to celebrate, because I thought your brother was dead, and he's alive; he was lost and now he's found.'* [5-second pause]

See your father presenting you with a really expensive new set of clothes and footwear, and placing the family ring on your finger. Visualise the amazingly rich and colourful spread of food in front of you . . . the music . . . the dancing . . . the laughter . . . all your friends and family gathered round celebrating your return. [Pause]

Spend some time now enjoying the atmosphere and extravagance of a real party, where love is the motivation, not money, and where you matter because you mean everything to your father. You've truly come home.

© Liz Babbs 2002

Leaders' Notes

This meditation may lead the participants into a recognition of their personal need. Participants should be offered the opportunity to talk to somebody in a supportive, caring conversation after the session if they would like to do so.

---

10. *Debrief*

Participants may need to verbalise their feelings as a means of debrief after the Ignatian exercise.

The labyrinth

11. *Labyrinth*

Participants are invited to take part in a 'mini-labyrinth' experience. Labyrinths create a symbolic journey and give participants the chance to unwind and to spend time with God. In the labyrinth there are different 'activity' stations in which the participants can spend time. This should provide an opportunity for reflection, for letting God take control, for meditation, prayer and response to God.

Leaders' Notes

This labyrinth taster is set out in four sections. It could be set up in different corners of the main space, but it would be ideal to use a separate room if possible, so that the stations can be set up before the beginning of the session. If using the same room, the stations should be kept covered until needed.

You can make a very simple kind of labyrinth using the four corners and centre of a room (see page 101). Participants move around in a clockwise direction at their own pace. They should not be rushed or interrupted throughout the exercise. It could be carried out in silence, or with soft music playing in the background.

It is suggested that at least 25 minutes be given for the labyrinth experience.

Leaders' Notes

The Introduction and Landmarks passages are written on card and placed at the entry to the labyrinth.

Introduction

As you enter the labyrinth you begin a journey – an encounter with God. Pause here and commit yourself to the journey. This is holy ground, so take off your shoes.

Landmarks

To journey . . .
you must travel.
To find . . .
you must lose yourself.
Exploration
risks change.
Are you a tourist or a pilgrim?

© Liz Babbs

(a) *Giving our stress to God*   Materials needed: a pile of sand, a bucket of water and a card with the poem written on it.

Think about your fears and worries one by one. See the heaviness they cause within your life. Spend as much time as you need to do this. Take hold of a handful of sand and imagine that all your fears and worries are represented by this sand.

When you are ready, release your sand into the water and

watch it sink to the bottom of the bucket. Do this as a symbol of releasing your burdens to God. Ask God to take control of these difficult aspects of your life. Trust in him. You need not be fearful again.

Poem

From the depths of my fears
You quench my soul with Your tears
You hold me
You enfold me
I'm secure in Your arms.

© Liz Babbs

Leaders' Notes

The instructions and the poem should be written on card and placed next to a pile of sand in labyrinth position 1. (Please see the suggested layout of the labyrinth at the end of this session.)

(b) *I'm made in God's image*   Materials needed: large mirror(s) and Bible verses on card.

We are all made in God's image and precious in the sight of God, no matter how we may feel about ourselves.

Bible passages

- Genesis 1:27: 'So God created man in his own image, in the image of God he created him; male and female he created them.'

- John 3:16: 'For God so loved the world that he gave his one and only Son, that whoever believes in him shall not perish but have eternal life.'

- 1 Corinthians 13:6: 'Love does not delight in evil but rejoices with the truth.'

Leaders' Notes

These Bible passages should be written on card and placed on or around the mirror(s) in labyrinth position 2.

(c) *Talking to God* Materials needed: 'Letter to a friend' and reply sheets for our response to God, with the Ephesians 3:20 passage printed on the top.

Read 'Letter to a friend' and then write a letter, poem or prayer, talking to God about your hopes and dreams for the future, using the reply sheets provided. Remember that God's power is awesome and that he has your best interests at heart.

Letter to a Friend

Yesterday, I saw you walking and laughing with your friends; I hoped that soon you'd want Me to walk along with you, too.

So I painted you a sunset to close your day and whispered a cool breeze to refresh you. I waited – you never called – I just kept on loving you.

As I watched you fall asleep last night, I wanted so much to touch you.

I spilled moonlight onto your face – trickling down your cheeks as so many tears have. You didn't even think of Me;

I wanted so much to comfort you.

The next day I exploded a brilliant sunrise into glorious morning for you.

But you woke up late and rushed off to work – you didn't even notice.

My sky became cloudy and My tears were in the rain.

I love you. Oh, if you'd only listen. I really love you.

I try to say it in the quiet of the green meadow and in the blue sky.

The wind whispers My love throughout the treetops and spills it into the vibrant colours of all the flowers.

I shout it to you in the thunder of the great waterfalls and compose love songs for birds to sing for you.

I warm you with the clothing of My sunshine and perfume the air with nature's sweet scent.

My love for you is deeper than any ocean and greater than any need in your heart. If you'd only realise how I care.

My Dad sends His love. I want you to meet Him – He cares, too.

Fathers are just that way. So, please call on Me soon.

No matter how long it takes. I'll wait – because I love you.
Your friend, Jesus

Author unknown

The following Bible passage is printed as the heading on the reply sheets. Pens are provided for a personal response to be written in the form of a statement, poem or prayer. Ephesians 3:20: '[God] is able to do immeasurably more than all we ask or imagine, according to his power that is at work within us.'

Leaders' Notes

The Bible verse is written at the top of the reply sheets. The 'Letter to a friend' and the instructions should be written on card and placed in labyrinth position 3.

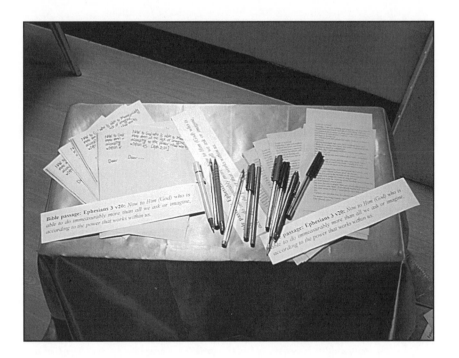

(d) *Exploring inner space*   Materials needed: candles and cushions to create a relaxed atmosphere, some incense and a cross (optional), juice and biscuits (optional), a large lighted candle, enough tea-light candles for each person placed on a tray of sand.

Instructions

As you enter the centre of the labyrinth, you enter holy space: your space to be with God, and God's space to be with you. Relax, rest a while and enjoy.

Meditation passages

In him [Jesus] and through faith in him we may approach God with freedom and confidence.

(Ephesians 3:12)

The best prayer is to rest in the goodness of God, knowing that that goodness can reach right down to our lowest depths of need.
Julian of Norwich – fourteenth century

Beholding this being – resting, rapt, in the vision and possession of so lofty a loveliness, growing to its likeness – what beauty can the soul yet lack? For this, the beauty supreme, the absolute and the primal, fashions its lovers to Beauty and makes them also worthy of love.
Plotinus (203–262 AD) *The Ennead*

What is this which shines on me and pierces my heart without hurting it? I shudder and am aflame at the same time: I shudder, because I am so similar to it. It is Wisdom, Wisdom itself which shines on me, breaking up my cloudiness, which yet covers me once more as I fall away from it through the darkness and rubble of my troubles.
St Augustine – fourth century

For it is the way of the perfect lover not only to love what he loves more than himself, but also in some sort to hate himself for the sake of what he loves. So you are to do with yourself. You must loathe and tire of all that goes on in your mind and your will unless it is God.
Anonymous, *The Cloud of Unknowing* – fourteenth century

And when I looked, I beheld God who spake with me. But if thou seekest to know that which I beheld, I can tell thee nothing, save that I beheld a fulness and a clearance, and felt them within me so abundantly that I can in no wise describe it, nor give any likeness thereof.

Angela of Foligno (1470–1540 AD)

Leaders' Notes

There should be sufficient space and time for people to relax and chill out in God's presence. Have the instructions and meditation passages printed out on cards and placed around the candles as a focus for people to pray and meditate upon. The 'Sands of Time' card should be placed near the main candle, which should be set in a deep tray filled with sand, to symbolise the sands of time. Burning incense, a cross, fruit juice and paper cups may be provided.

Instructions

Take a small candle and light it, using the larger one, as a response to God, allowing his light always to light up the journey you are on.

Sands of Time

And so Lord
Somewhere in the distance we meet.
Is it eternity or some future time?
Is there a nowness about it, a separation and beyond
an otherness but togetherness
Walking hand in hand
Across the sands of time?

© Liz Babbs

12. *Tasting the good things of God*

When participants have completed the labyrinth, the leaders invite them to gather around the candle in the centre of the room. The wrapped parcel that was used at the beginning of the session is unwrapped, and the chocolates are passed around.

The leader explains that we are all on a journey and on that journey we can miss the good things and the important things of God along the way. We can even miss meeting God. At the close of this activity the leader prays a simple prayer, asking God to help and guide participants on their journey towards him.

13. *Homework*

The leader asks each member of the group to bring a photo of them- selves as a young child for use during an activity next week.

Shopping list

Section 1

- A wrapped box of chocolates

- A CD of chart music

Section 2

- Enough paper, pens, pencils and felt-tip pens for everyone

Section 3

- Strips of coloured paper/card – at least two or three for each member of the group

- A pre-made 'weave' example

Section 4

- Paper and pens for each group

Section 11

- Labyrinth

- Introduction passages written/printed out on card

(a)

- A pile of silver sand

- A large bucket/container of water

- Poem and instructions written/printed out on card

(b)

- A large mirror or mirrors

- Bible passages written/printed out on card (Genesis 1:27; John 3:16; 1 Corinthians 13:6)

- Instructions written/printed out on card

(c)

- Headed paper with Ephesians 3:20 written/printed at the top

- Pens

- 'Letter to a friend' and instructions written/printed on card

(d)

- Large candle

- Tea lights (one for each person)

- A tray of silver sand

- A cross and incense (optional)

- Cushions

- Juice and biscuits (optional)

- Bible passage, meditation passages and instructions written/ printed out on card

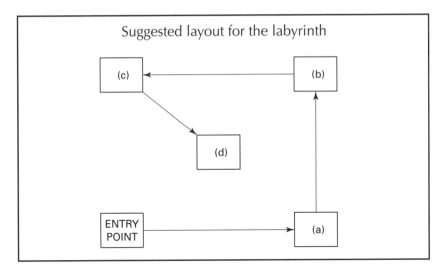

Suggested layout for the labyrinth

Running order – crib sheet

1. Pass the parcel

2. Pictures

3. Word pictures of God

4. Spiritual experiences

5. Weaving

6. My story

7. The Prodigal Son (story on CD)

8. Role plays

9. Exploration of the Prodigal (meditation on CD)

10. Debrief

11. Labyrinth

12. Tasting the good things of God

13. Homework

SESSION 6

The Journey to the Future

Key concepts: hopes and dreams, the future, eternity

This final session encourages the group to look at the future and their mortality and to explore Christian concepts of eternity. It enables the group to face up to the passing of time and to appreciate the concept of God's presence with us.

Leaders' Notes

As the group arrive, a leader collects the childhood photos that the participants were asked to bring with them. The leaders should all bring photos too. If some participants haven't brought pictures they should not be made to feel embarrassed.

There should be a Christian symbol such as a wooden cross in the centre of the room throughout this session.

Introduction to the journey

1. *Photographs*

The personal photos are placed on the floor and the group are invited to walk around them and look at them. Participants attempt to guess which photo belongs to which person.

 The group then move into sets. This exercise can be used to trigger a general discussion in the sets on such subjects as:

- What aspects of ageing have you struggled with most?

- How do you think your appearance will change in the future?

- How do you think your personality will change in the years to come?

- Do negative and positive experiences influence the way in which we mature?

- Are you optimistic or pessimistic about the future?

2. *Timeless*

While remaining in their sets people are asked to remove their watches and put them in their pockets, or on a table provided. All of the clocks in the room are covered. People find a space in which to lie down or relax. The leader reads the 'Silence' meditation.

Silence

Silence is making friends with time. It does not fight it or waste it, it refuses to run after it.

Silence floats free with time, letting the pattern of the moments unfold at its own pace . . .

In silence we break the hold time has on us, and accept, in practice, that our true home is eternity.

3. *Time lines*

The sets move back into one group. The leader introduces the challenge of measuring how many hours we spend doing various things in a week. The participants are encouraged to consider how precious time is, and how we are often bound by it, how we can waste it or even wish it away!

A time chart (see below) is handed out to each group member, and the participants are invited to work out how they spend their 168 hours each week. There are 42 segments in the pie chart, each representing four hours. The pie chart should be shaded in different colours to represent different activities (e.g. pink for sleeping, brown for working, blue for eating, green for hobbies, etc.). Reassure people that they won't have to show their chart to others in the group!

Time Chart

Each segment represents four hours

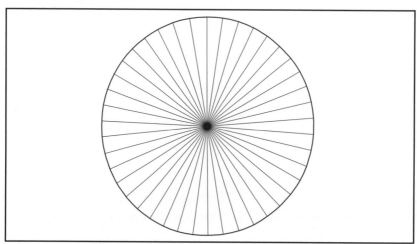

Participants are given some time to shade in the chart, and to use this exercise as a personal audit of their lives. They can add their own categories to the chart if they wish (e.g. homework, TV viewing).

Leaders' Notes

This exercise could take ten minutes or more. It should not be rushed. Quiet music could be played in the background. This is not only a mathematical exercise but also an important opportunity to reflect on our priorities in life.

4. *Blind guides*

The aim of this exercise is to demonstrate that many voices clamour for our attention in life, but some can mislead us. Christians believe that we need to listen for God's voice above all others.

The group stand in a circle. One person is asked to volunteer to be the 'traveller'. The person is blindfolded and turned around a couple

of times. A 'good guide' is then chosen from the group. Their voice will guide the 'traveller' safe home. The 'good guide' says, 'I am the good guide. Listen for my voice.' Three 'blind guides' are then selected silently from around the circle.

All four guides then shout instructions to the 'traveller', who must only follow the advice of the 'good guide'. The aim is for the 'traveller' to move around the circle and to reach the voice of the 'good guide'. There should be various obstacles in the way, e.g. leaders standing in the way of the 'traveller'.

The exercise is repeated a couple of times, with others taking the part of the 'traveller' and the four guides.

The group move back into sets, where their leaders trigger discussion about which voices clamour for attention in our lives. Participants are invited to share honestly about their hopes and fears for the future. Do they have any sense of their long-term direction? Where are they headed in five, ten or twenty years' time? The set leaders should endeavour to raise such questions as: 'Which voices are guiding you?' 'Who do you trust?' 'Where are you headed?'

Leaders' Notes

Leaders may want to refer participants who have specific questions about New Age or occult experiences to the Reachout Trust, an organisation working with enquirers to help them find salvation through Christ.

Reachout Trust
24 Ormond Road
Richmond TW10 6TH

Tel: 020 83327785
Fax: 020 83320286
Email: info@reachouttrust.org

5. *Quotable quotes*

Still working in sets, the following list of quotes is handed to each participant.

- I hope I'm old before I die. (Robbie Williams, British singer)

- I hope I die before I'm old. (Roger Daltry, British singer and actor)

- The world is like an amusement park . . . some people have been on the ride for a long time and they begin to question 'Is this real or is this just a ride?' And other people have remembered and they come back to us and they say, 'Hey, don't worry, don't be afraid ever, because this is just a ride.' (Bill Hicks, US comedian)

- Life is just one damned thing after another. (Elbert Hubbard, US writer)

- Life is like a sewer. What you get out of it depends on what you put into it. (Tom Lehrer, lecturer and songwriter)

- Life is what happens to you while you're busy making other plans. (John Lennon, British rock musician)

- As our life is very short, so it is very miserable and therefore it is well it is short. (Jeremy Taylor, English Anglican theologian)

- Most people get a fair amount of fun out of their lives, but on balance life is suffering and only the very young or the very foolish imagine otherwise. (George Orwell, British novelist)

- Life is not a spectacle or a feast; it is a predicament. (George Santayana, US philosopher)

- Time and tide wait for no man. (Proverb)

- And so, from hour to hour, we ripe and ripe; And then, from hour to hour, we rot and rot; And thereby hangs a tale. (William Shakespeare)

- He had decided to live forever, or die in the attempt. (Joseph Heller, US novelist)

- There are only three events in a man's life; birth, life and death; he is not conscious of being born, he dies in pain and he forgets to live. (Jean de La Bruyere, French satirist)

- I never think of the future. It comes soon enough. (Albert Einstein, German born US physicist)

- God has forgotten me. (Jeanne Calment, French woman, 120 years old)

- Dost thou love life? Then do not squander time, for that's the stuff life is made of. (Benjamin Franklin, US scientist and statesman)

Set members are invited to spend a few minutes mulling over their list of quotes, giving each one a score (0 for the one they least agree with, and 10 for the one they most agree with). Music could be played during this time.

Set members share their scores and say why they agree with some statements more than others. They are then invited to make up their own personal 'quotable quote' about the passing of time. These are shared with the rest of the set and the set leader writes them on a long piece of paper with a felt-tip pen.

Looking forward

6. My story

The large group reconvenes. Leaders share testimony of how God has helped them and how they have known his guidance over the years. They also talk of the way in which their confidence for the future is based on trusting God rather than people.

7. Sands of time

A pile of silver sand and some small plastic or silver plates are placed in the centre of the large group. Members are invited to move to the centre and collect a plate with a couple of handfuls of sand on it.

The participants are then invited to spend a few moments

running the sand through their fingers and meditating on 'the sands of time'.

During this exercise the 'Seasons Come and Go' meditation is played from the *Essence* CD, track 13. This activity is designed to initiate thoughts about time and eternity, mortality and immortality.

Seasons Come and Go

The seasons come and go,
And I note their passing.
The cold grey of winter
Becomes the sunshine of spring.
The bare trees of December
Are filled by the lush green leaves of June.

The seasons of history come and go,
Empires fall away
And leaders process
Towards obscurity.
Fashions change,
Philosophies wither,
Causes fade away.

The seasons of my life
Come and go.
Yesterday I ran like a child
With the optimism of youth.
But time moves on.

The seasons come and go
But you are still here,
Lord of the seasons.
I rest again in the changeless season
Of your eternal faithfulness.

© Rob Frost

As the music continues, the following passage should be read out at this point.

Romans 8:31–39

What, then, shall we say in response to this? If God is for us, who can be against us? He who did not spare his own Son, but gave him up for us all – how will he not also, along with him, graciously give us all things? Who will bring any charge against those whom God has chosen? It is God who justifies. Who is he that condemns? Christ Jesus, who died – more than that, who was raised to life – is at the right hand of God and is also interceding for us. Who shall separate us from the love of Christ? Shall trouble or hardship or persecution or famine or nakedness or danger or sword? As it is written: 'For your sake we face death all day long; we are considered as sheep to be slaughtered.'

No, in all these things we are more than conquerors through him who loved us. For I am convinced that neither death nor life, neither angels nor demons, neither the present nor the future, nor any powers, neither height nor depth, nor anything else in all creation, will be able to separate us from the love of God that is in Christ Jesus our Lord.

8. *Here for a season*

The group leader then invites each group member, if they wish, to smooth out their sand, and to mark their initials in the sand.

Track 14, 'The Journey', from the *Essence* CD is then played. 🎵

The Journey

The journeys we make express who we are:
We journey to be together
We journey to escape
We journey to grow up
We journey to experience
We journey to share
We journey to change things
We journey to be free
We journey to discover
We journey to find ourselves
We journey to come home

But until we find our home in You
our journey is incomplete.

© Liz Babbs

After this the group members are invited, if they wish, to slowly smooth out their initials as a symbol of the transience of their own life.

9. *Ribbons of hope*

A length of thick rope is laid out down the middle of the room and ribbons are placed in several piles around the room. The leader explains that one end of the rope represents a positive view of life, the other end a negative perspective.

One by one each person takes a piece of ribbon from one of the piles around the room. They then tie the ribbon to the rope at a point that represents their level of optimism or pessimism about the future. This is done in silence. (They may take more than one ribbon and attach them to different places on the rope, if they feel that this is more appropriate.)

☺   Once everyone's ribbon is in place the group divide into their sets
     to share why they placed their ribbon(s) in a certain position along
the rope. The participants are then asked to share some of their hopes
and fears for the future.

     One of the leaders introduces Revelation 22:1–5 by saying that
this passage epitomises Christian hope.

Revelation 22:1–5

Then the angel showed me the river of the water of life, as clear as crystal, flowing from the throne of God and of the Lamb down the middle of the great street of the city. On each side of the river stood the tree of life, bearing twelve crops of fruit, yielding its fruit every month. And the leaves of the tree are for the healing of the nations. No longer will there be any curse. The throne of God and of the Lamb will be in the city, and his servants will serve him. They will see his face, and his name will be on their foreheads. There will be no more night. They will not need the light of a lamp or the light of the sun, for the Lord God will give them light. And they will reign for ever and ever.

10. *The love feast*

Leaders' Notes

The bread to be shared at the love feast can be any kind of small loaf, but currant loaves or spiced buns would more closely resemble the loaves used by Christian pilgrims in medieval times.

We recommend that this session be brought to a close with a time of sharing of bread and fruit juice or water. It is important that everyone present realises that this is not a Holy Communion, but a love feast – a sharing of our belonging to each other and ultimately to God.

As the bread is passed around, each person tears off a piece and eats it. No words are spoken. This sharing of the loaf is a symbol of our belonging to one another because we all belong to the one who is the Bread of Life. This time should be a time of silent encouragement, support and love. We can sometimes say more with our silence than with our words.

Next the 'common cup' is passed around. All the participants

drink from the same cup as a symbol of their unity. This is also done
in silence.

11. *Footprints*

The leader thanks the group for their participation in *Essence*. If any
have placed their watches on the table, they should reclaim them
now. The leader explains that there will be an opportunity after the
close of the session for people to talk individually with leaders about
how they could become a committed Christian. Or they could be
invited to a special guest service or testimony evening or further
course in which the Christian gospel of repentance, forgiveness and
salvation is explained in simple terms.

The leader then invites the participants to place their portion of
sand next to the cross as a symbol of God's ownership of all things.

Afterwards the group leader reads out the 'Footprints' text and asks
God's blessing on the continuing spiritual journey of each group
member.

Footprints

*One night I dreamed a dream. I was walking along the beach with
my Lord. Across the dark sky flashed scenes from my life. For each
scene, I noticed two sets of footprints in the sand, one belonging
to me and one to my Lord.*

*When the last scene of my life shot before me I noticed that
many times along the path of my life there was only one set of footprints. I realised that this was at the lowest and saddest times of my
life. This always bothered me and I questioned the Lord about my
dilemma.*

*'Lord, You told me when I decided to follow You, You would
walk with me all the way. But I'm aware that during the most
troublesome times of my life there is only one set of footprints.
I just don't understand why, when I need You most, You leave
me.'*

*He whispered, 'My precious child, I love you and will never,
ever leave you during your trials and testings. When you saw only
one set of footprints it was then that I carried you.'*

Leaders' Notes

Leaders may want to hand out copies of 'Footprints' for the participants to take home.

Shopping list

Section 2

- Cloths to cover up all clocks

Section 3

- Felt-tip pens
- Time charts printed onto paper

Section 4

- A blindfold

Section 5

- A copy of the list of quotable quotes for each set
- A large piece of paper for each set
- Marker pens

Section 7

- A large bowl or bucket
- Sand (silver sand from B & Q is the best)
- A foil tray or paper plates for each person

Section 9

- A long length of thick rope
- A piece of ribbon for each person, plus a few spare

Section 10

- Bread and fruit juice (or mineral water) to share
- A copy of 'Footprints' for each person
- A wooden cross

Running order – crib sheet

 1. Photograph

 2. Timeless

3. Time lines

 4. Blind guides

 5. Quotable quotes

6. My story

7. Sands of time (meditation on CD)   ♫

8. Here for a season (meditation on CD)   ♫

9. Ribbons of hope

10. The love feast

11. Footprints

Feedback and Suggestions

We would appreciate feedback and suggestions following your experience of using *Essence.* Please send any feedback to:

Share Jesus International
Tolverne Road
Raynes Park
London SW20 8RA

Tel: 020 8944 5678 (ask for the *Essence* desk)
Email: essence@sharejesusinternational.com

Updates and training information will be available on our website: www.sharejesusinternational.com

Publication Copyright List

- 'Hand' meditation – original author unknown © adapted by Martha Keys Barker and Patricia Beall. Celebration Services International Ltd 1973,1977.

- 'Palms Up, Palms Down' meditation – adapted by Liz Babbs from Richard Foster's, *Celebration of Discipline* (Hodder & Stoughton 1980).

- 'Renew Me, Lord' meditation – taken from the book *Out of the Depths* by Liz Babbs (Eagle 2001), p. 32.

- 'Make me a channel of Your peace' – Sebasian Temple © Franciscan Communications 1967.

- Theodore Roosevelt quote, *The Book of Naturalists* (Princeton University Press 1988) © William Beebe.

- 'Silence' meditation – *Meditations on Silence* (Dorling Kindersley 1995) © Sister Wendy Beckett, p. 34.

- Extract taken from the song 'The Lord's my Shepherd' by Stuart Townend. Copyright © 1996 Thankyou Music. Adm. by worshiptogether.com songs excl. UK & Europe, adm. by Kingsway Music.tym@kingway.co.uk Used by permission.

Every effort has been made to gain copyright permission for use of other materials within this *Essence* manual and the accompanying CD.

CD Track Listing

1. Stones – meditation (4.03 mins)

Read by Liz Babbs.
Music taken from the album: The Journey, Simeon Wood and John Gerighty, track 1 'First Journey' (Eagle 0863471218).

2. The Lord's My Shepherd – song (3.25 mins)

Song by Stuart Townend © 1996 Thankyou Music.
Taken from the album: Celtic Expressions Vol. 3, Joanne Hogg (Kingsway KMCD2254).

3. Palms Up, Palms Down – meditation (4.30 mins)

Read by Liz Babbs from Richard Foster's Celebration of Discipline (used by permission of Hodder & Stoughton).
Music taken from the album: Impressions, Simeon Wood and John Gerighty, track 6 'Claire de Lune' (Eagle 0863471005).

4. Relax and Be – relaxation/meditation (4.12 mins)

© Rob Frost 2002.
Music taken from the album: Impressions, Simeon Wood and John Gerighty, track 4 'The Swan' (Eagle 0863471005).

5. Natural Sounds (5.53 mins)

Used by permission of Premier Radio.

6. How We Break the World! – meditation (5.08 mins)

© Rob Frost.
Music taken from the album: Celtic Roots and Rhythms, Nick and Anita Haigh, track 6 'Strange Land' (ICC ICCD47330).

7. Renew Me Lord – meditation (1.15 mins)

Read by Liz Babbs from Out of the Depths © Eagle 2001.
Music taken from the album: Grace Instrumental, Labyrinth, Baker/Birch, track 1 'Inward Journey' (Proost PRCD06).

8. The Gentle Healer – song (2.02 mins)

Taken from the album: The Life by Michael Card © Sparrow/EMI (Sparrow SPD 1171).

9. Such Love – meditation (4.35 mins)

Read by Liz Babbs.
Taken from Out of the Depths audio cassette, Liz Babbs (Eagle 0863474063).

10. The Prodigal – story 1 (3.59 mins)

Read and written by Rob Lacey © 1998.

11. The Prodigal – story 2 (3.45 mins)

Written by Rob Lacey © 1998.

12. The Prodigal – meditation (7.20 mins)

Read and written by Liz Babbs © 2002.

13. The Seasons Come and Go – meditation (3.15 mins)

Read by Liz Babbs © Rob Frost.
Music taken from the album: Whispers of Creation Inspirational Melodies, Simeon Wood and John Gerighty, track 10 'Beautiful Hollow by the Broad Bay' (Eagle 086347151).

14. The Journey – meditation (4.52 mins)

Music taken from the album: A Still Small Voice, John Gerighty, track 2 'A Still Small Voice' (Eagle 0863473350).